BRINGING IT OUT I[

Domestic Violence in Northern Ireland

MONICA MCWILLIAMS

and

JOAN MCKIERNAN

BRINGING IT OUT IN THE OPEN:
Domestic Violence in Northern Ireland

A study commissioned by the

Department of Health and Social Services

(Northern Ireland)

MONICA MCWILLIAMS and JOAN MCKIERNAN

Centre for Research on Women

University of Ulster

BELFAST: HMSO

1993

ISBN 0 337 07824 6

Printed in the United Kingdom for HMSO
Dd. 0309513. C3. 3/95.

CONTENTS

Acknowledgements

We should like to thank all those groups and individuals, throughout Northern Ireland who participated in this research project. In particular, we acknowledge the support given by the Northern Ireland Women's Aid Federation who provided access to their refuges and by the many refuge workers who gave us such a warm welcome and contributed many important insights from their long experience in supporting abused women. We appreciate the valuable assistance given by Professor Celia Davies, Director of the Centre for Research on Women in the University of Ulster. Jalna Hanmer took on the task of consultant to the project, giving us the benefit of her long experience in this field. We are grateful to Lorraine Brownlie for her work in transcribing endless hours of tapes, Morag Stark for her administrative and secretarial assistance and Mike Morrissey and Paul Brotherton who provided technical assistance to the project.

Thanks are due to the many statutory and voluntary personnel, solicitors, and members of women's and community groups who so willingly gave their time to discuss the issue of domestic violence, to help us contact women, and to provide information and retrieve data for the project. A number of representatives from both the statutory and voluntary sector agreed to serve on the project's steering committee. We thank them for their support: Celia Davies, Pauline Ginnity, Margo Heskett, Felicity McCartney, Elizabeth McClatchey, Eithne McLaughlin, Karen McMinn, Liz McWhirter, Edis Nicholl and Joe Wright.

But most important, we are grateful to the women themselves who opened up their homes and their hearts to share their pain, their disappointment, their anger – and their hopes for the future. They showed great determination and courage in taking this crucial step toward bringing domestic violence "out in the open".

This study was commissioned by the Department of Health and Social Services. However, the opinions and recommendations expressed in the report are the responsibility of the researchers and not the Department.

MONICA MCWILLIAMS
Senior Lecturer in Social Policy
University of Ulster

JOAN MCKIERNAN
Research Officer,
Centre for Research on Women
University of Ulster

EXECUTIVE SUMMARY

This book sets out the findings of a major study of domestic violence in Northern Ireland involving both help-seekers and help-providers. It is based on in-depth interviews with 56 women who had sought help in relation to domestic violence and includes 120 interviews with a wide range of service providers, covering health and social service professionals, those working in Women's Aid and in other voluntary organisations as well as the police, Probation Service and the Housing Executive. An extensive literature in the United Kingdom, the USA and elsewhere is reviewed, paying particular attention to the contribution that health and social service professionals have made, and to the problems that have arisen in this area.

As far as women's experience of domestic violence is concerned, findings confirm its seriousness. By domestic violence is meant repeated physical abuse which can threaten women's health and put their lives at risk. It is damage to their physical well-being, to their sense of self-worth and ability to take control of their lives. It can have serious, sometimes long-term effects on children. There is no doubt that the accounts which are reported here make harrowing and salutory reading.

A complex picture of statutory service provision emerged from the study because no single agency has clear responsibility in this area. Interviews show that there is an absence of guidelines and of any coherent recording of domestic violence. Clearly there is good practice, and examples of this are recorded. Equally clearly however, domestic violence is often minimised or missed altogether, or viewed with embarrassment as an invasion of privacy, or with alarm as an extension to an already heavy workload.

Voluntary sector provision in this area comes from a number of groups, but most notably from Women's Aid, both through its refuges and its advice and support services. The philosophy underlying this provision stresses the need to empower women and give them real choice.

A Northern Ireland dimension is noted in all of this insofar as responses of both help-seekers and help-providers are often coloured by traditional beliefs that value the maintenance of the family and reinforce the subordinate position of women in it. The violence of 'The Troubles' also perhaps serves to overshadow domestic violence.

Reviewing the findings both from the point of view of help-seekers and help-providers, the conclusions reaffirm the seriousness of domestic violence and the importance of developing a consistent policy that responds to domestic violence as a problem in its own right. There are 13 recommendations in all (see page 84). These highlight the need for an overall policy framework, for training, for guidelines and inter-agency liaison. A new community based advocacy service is among the major suggestions, as is a broad based programme of public education. Annexes elaborate on some of these recommendations and also describe key initiatives taken elsewhere to deal with domestic violence. The project was designed to be preliminary to an action intervention, and the importance of getting this under way as soon as possible is emphasised.

ONE

Introduction

Background to the Study

The origins of this project lie in a recommendation to the Home Office that the health and social service professions should examine more effective ways of dealing with those experiencing domestic violence. This recommendation, made as a result of an extensive research review (Smith 1989), was taken up by the Ministerial Group on Women's Issues and resulted in a proposal to mount a number of three-year demonstration projects in different parts of the United Kingdom, each designed to explore and test the effectiveness of different kinds of skilled interventions which could be made by professionals.

Local consideration of this proposal led to the rapid realisation that, contrary to the position in Britain, very little was known about the range of formal agencies and the informal structures which are brought into play in Northern Ireland when domestic violence occurs. It was agreed that the optimal strategy was to carry out an initial information-gathering exercise to establish some of the key parameters for a Northern Ireland intervention project. In this way the eventual intervention could be based not solely on existing literature from other settings, but also on the direct insights of local research. Consequently the DHSS commissioned the research on which this report is based.

A twelve-month period was set in which the researchers would (a) gather information from women who had been subject to domestic violence, exploring the nature of that violence and the patterns of helpseeking as they emerged in the Northern Ireland context and (b) gather information on the perceptions and experience of the various professional groups and agencies in the statutory and voluntary sectors who currently offer a response to domestic violence. It was recognised that while the focus of this part of the enquiry would largely be with health and social services professionals in the statutory sector and with Women's Aid in the voluntary sector, a wide range of other agencies would also need to be contacted, the police, the courts, the probation services, the Housing Executive and others. As the first study of service response to domestic violence directly in Northern Ireland it was felt important that the net was cast as widely as possible.

Definition

For the purposes of this project, domestic violence has been defined as "the intentional physical abuse of a woman in a way that causes pain or injury or the threat of physical abuse by the male partner with whom she lives or has lived" (Montgomery and Bell 1986). As a working definition this focuses on three key aspects: that it is most frequently directed against women by men; that it is intentional; and that it involves physical aggression. This definition forms the starting point for the project, although it is recognised that other forms of sexual and mental abuse may co-exist and may be equally serious.

Some might argue that research on the subject of domestic violence should include these other forms of violence. However, to expand the definition in this way would make the task unmanageable and run the risk of losing the particular focus that violence against women in relationships requires, if it is to be effectively addressed. Whilst the findings of prevalent studies show a small proportion of women being violent to men, the focus of our report is on women, reflecting this research showing that the vast majority of violence in relationships is from men to women. The research is not confined, however, to legally married couples since it includes couples who are cohabiting and women who have been living apart from their partners. It is acknowledged also that the term domestic violence can be misleading since it both assumes an element of neutrality in relation to the focus of the violence and does not highlight sufficiently the fact that serious assaults can take place outside of the domestic setting and often long after the woman has separated from her partner. None the less, it is the most popularly known term and will be used extensively in this book.

Policy Content

Domestic violence is not something new. As long ago as the four-teenth century, reference was made to a case of a woman seeking refuge from her abusive husband. It was not, however, until 1878 that legislation was introduced accepting domestic violence as grounds for an official separation. Present social policy (as oppsed to legislative) approaches on domestic violence can be traced back only to 1975, with the Parliamentary Select Committee on Vio-lence in Marriage. This Committee emerged in the wake of the very considerable public recognition that the women's movement, and particularly Women's Aid, had gained for work on domestic vio-lence. It endorsed many of the principles behind Womens Aid's refuge provision and its emphasis on self help. Expressing alarm at "the ignorance and apparent apathy of some Government Depart-ments and individual Ministers towards the extent of marital vio-lence" (cited in Dobash and Dobash 1992:121), the final report of the Select Committee made three important recommendations con-cerning housing and safety. In the following sessions of Parliament, legislation was passed putting these into effect in England and Wales, and then later in Scotland and Northern Ireland. The 1976 Domestic Violence and Matrimonial Proceedings Act and the 1978 Domestic Proceedings and Magistrates Court Act in England two years later became the Domestic Proceedings (NI) Order 1980. The Order gave women the right to occupy the matrimonial home and provided wives with protection and exclusion orders against their husbands. In 1984, the legislation was extended to cover co-habitees. These civil orders for the first time gave the police a clearly defined role in intervention and in facilitating the enforcement of the law. Their role was strengthened in Northern Ireland by the power of arrest attached to all relevant orders made in the Magistrates Court. As a consequence, however, of recent judicial difficulties with this legislation, the Family Law (Northern Ireland) Order proposed in 1992 contains provisions making breaches of protection or exclu-sion orders a criminal offence.

The Select Committee also emphasised the responsibility of local authorities to provide women, who have left their homes because of violence, with temporary accommodation. In order for abused women to receive priority status for rehousing, the government introduced the Housing (Homeless) Persons Act in 1977 in Britain. This was finally introduced into Northern Ireland, as the Housing Order (NI), 1988.

In the 1980s, domestic violence again came to the attention of government through the Women's National Commission. This advisory group to government produced a report in 1985 recommending better police training and more inter-agency liaison. They also called for adequate funding for refuges and drew attention to the housing needs of women. In response to this report, the Home Office issued a circular in 1986 to all Police Chief Officers in England and Wales, which stated that the over-riding concern in dealing with domestic violence was to ensure the safety of victims and to reduce the risk of further violence. This was to form the basis for new guidelines on domestic violence which were to be introduced by the various police forces throughout the United Kingdom and the Royal Ulster Constabulary issued its own Force Order (7/91) on domestic violence in March 1991.

In 1992, a further Select Committee on domestic violence was established to receive submissions from those carrying out work in this area in England and Wales. It has held several hearings to date and has published its first report on the subject.

The role of the police, the courts and housing in the potential alleviation of domestic violence has thus been the focus of much policy development in recent years. The role which the health and social service professions can play has attracted much less attention. All of this forms the backdrop to this project.

Extent of Domestic Violence

Despite the enormous amount of research that has been done on domestic violence and the activities of pressure groups since the 1970s, it is still impossible to make an accurate statement on the prevalence of domestic violence. This is partly to do with the limitations of surveys (which we discuss in Chapter Two). It is also to do with the lack of consistency in recording of domestic violence, something which emerges in other research and which, as will be seen, was widespread also in Northern Ireland.

We made considerable efforts to locate potential sources of statistical data and to discuss their compilation and recording with this problem in mind. Every one of the sources had limitations, but as some rough initial indication we can note that in 1991/92 in Northern Ireland,

- excluding deaths attributable to the Troubles, there were 25 homicides, 10 of which resulted from domestic violence
- there were over 2,800 domestic disputes recorded by the RUC
- there were 2,500 personal protection orders granted to women
- there were over 2,300 exclusion orders granted to women
- over 1,000 women, together with over 2,000 children, came to Women's Aid looking for accommodation
- nearly 1,400 women came to Women's Aid for information and support
- a total of 416 applications for rehousing cited domestic violence as the reason for homelessness and more than 1,300 more cited marital dispute.

A local community survey of women's health in the Ardoyne area of North Belfast found that domestic violence was reported to affect the lives of 27 per cent – this is more than one in four women (Ardoyne Women's Research Project 1992).

This project itself has become testimony to the seriousness of domestic violence. Whilst the research was being carried out, we were provided with evidence of the deaths of two women in the areas in which we were working. One of these women was five months pregnant and the other was the mother of six children – both their partners have been charged with manslaughter. During an interview in a hospital within our sample area, we were told of a female patient who had recently been admitted to intensive care after being thrown down the stairs by her husband. Her neck was broken in the fall and she will be permanently paralysed.

Our interviews with women show the horror of domestic violence both for those experiencing it and those dealing with it. It is very much a matter of life or death. The problem arises when it is not recognised as such – when it is ignored, when it is seen as a private matter between husband and wife, when it is not acknowledged that such traumatic events go on day and daily behind the closed doors of family homes. The reality of domestic violence flies in the face of what we want to believe about families. This may be particularly the case in rural areas where claims are made about close family networks and where partners are perceived to support each other rather than hurt each other. This image of the "happy family" or the pretence of "keeping the side up" for the sake of appearances can become a major problem in itself. It may prove to be a barrier in telling anyone – particularly someone outside the family who may be in a position to help. It may also be influential in the extent to which "outsiders" feel it is legitimate to ask about domestic violence. In other words, the "asking" and the "telling" are part of a complex process and need to be recognised as such by all concerned. It was imperative that recognition of this informed the methodology of the research.

Research Design

The project aims to make an assessment of the helpseeking process of women who have experienced domestic violence in Northern Ireland and to appraise the responses of the various agencies with whom abused women came into contact. The intention was to collect baseline data on the relevant dimensions of domestic violence and to assess the extent to which the helpseeking process differed from Great Britain and elsewhere. The design started from four assumptions. The first was that women who experience domestic violence are not passive victims but actively seek help and support through informal and formal networks and experience a process of becoming or not becoming a client, the patterns of which can be documented. The second was that professionals will react to domestic violence in ways affected by their backgrounds and training, their workloads, policies and priorities as shaped by the agencies in which they are employed. The third assumption was that the perspective of the help-providers and in particular help-seekers is crucial to the success of any intervention in this area. The fourth and final assumption was that any understanding of help-seeking and help-provision in Northern Ireland must take account of the varying contexts in which assistance is potentially sought and delivered.

There were two stages of data collection. The first involved in-depth interviews with women who had recent experience of domestic violence, the second involved the help-providers and focused on professional practice in relation to domestic violence. The second phase was designed to build on the first so that the various agencies would have the opportunity to respond to the specific problems which the women had encountered.

In order to assess the potential impact of specific local factors, the research on help-providers focused on two localities, one urban area located in the Eastern Health and Social Services Board, and a rural area located in the Western Health and Social Services Board. Interviews were carried out in a predominantly Catholic area and a predominantly Protestant area in both localities in order to assess whether there were any significant differences amongst the help-seekers and the help-providers in relation to the religious/political divide. The target areas were also chosen on the basis of the research team's strong network of contacts with community organisations and women's groups in these locations. The sample of help-seekers was drawn from the target areas as well as from a number of other areas in Northern Ireland (see Table 1).

It was clear from the outset that there could be no question of convenient sampling frames in which to find victims of domestic violence. Such samples have to be assembled through a process of negotiation and building trust. The first step was to generate a sample of women in refuges. The Northern Ireland Women's Aid Federation, together with a number of other providers of sheltered accommodation, agreed to facilitate the process of access to the refuges and to liaise with the researchers as required. A considerable amount of time was spent in discussing the project with refuge workers as well as with groups of women living in the refuges so that the aims of the project could be explained before any interviews were carried out. It is important to note that gaining access to a refuge requires a good deal of sensitivity on the part of those seeking information from outside. Not only must the research be seen as having some value but the researchers themselves need to spend time developing trust with all those concerned. Twenty-two women from a total of five refuges were ultimately included in the study.

We then turned to women in the community. This involved intricate and in-depth networking with a variety of intermediary bodies. A number of solicitors throughout Northern Ireland were contacted. Solicitors were thought to be potentially useful for meeting middle class women who might not go to other sources of help. We discussed the project with solicitors and sent letters and forms to be used for women clients for whom domestic violence was an issue. The solicitors agreed to co-operate and many welcomed the project as a much needed development. Interviews were then conducted with women who were referred through solicitors. Contacts in the sample areas were developed principally through local women's and community groups and we spent considerable time in discussing domestic violence with groups of women in their own homes. This enabled the project to have a deeper understanding of the attitudes of women in a local community towards social and health professionals and the barriers to help-seeking that currently exist.

In order to assess the particular problems women in the Traveller community might face, we met Traveller women both in refuges and in the Glen Road site. This access was made possible through the community worker attached to the Travellers. While we were not able to interview any Asian women, workers attached to the Chinese Welfare Association discussed the obstacles facing Asian women living in Northern Ireland. Contacts were also pursued with voluntary groups such as Safer Towns, Victim Support, and local community organisations who had an interest in the issue of domestic violence in the sample areas. Access to the various voluntary groups in the rural locality was initiated through a Community Development worker. Staff of several voluntary groups who had experience in working with victims of domestic violence assisted in locating women who agreed to be interviewed. Finally, the researchers attended and addressed public meetings and conferences such as the Women's Information Days in different communities to explain the work of the project. A special leaflet was produced for use at these meetings and for other occasions.

These various techniques meant that we met and talked to 76 women in either individual or group discussions. Sixty-four women agreed to in-depth interviews. Of these women 56 have been used for analysis for this study. Those not included in the sample were women who came to Northern Ireland after their relationships were ended and were not in previous contact with help-providers in Northern Ireland, and some Traveller women who discussed particular experiences for their group. Further details of the sample are set out in Annex 1.

The second stage of the project involved appropriate individuals from both the voluntary and statutory agencies. Within the statutory sector, three different levels of management were identified and targeted for interviews. The interviewees included: those employed in the areas where our samples were located; those employed at the unit of management level; and those employed in a managerial capacity at Board Level. General practitioners, social workers, health visitors, community psychiatric nurses and others were included. The relevant hospitals within the two localities were also included and interviews were conducted with the consultants and senior nursing staff in the respective accident and emergency departments. Details of numbers and locations of staff are shown in Annex 1. Within the voluntary sector, interviews were also conducted with a wide range of voluntary and informal help providers in the areas being studied and at headquarter level. The selection here was influenced by the responses of the women saying what agencies they had contacted. Further details again appear in Annex 1. In all, a total of 120 help-providers were interviewed as part of this study.

Since the role of the Housing Executive has increased in importance as providers of accommodation and is, for many women, the first point of contact in the process of help seeking, we interviewed Housing Executive officials in the relevant areas to discuss their guidelines and practice. We also met with Royal Ulster Constabulary (R.U.C.) personnel responsible for domestic violence liaison work at headquarters level and also with local police members of the C.A.R.E. Team in one of the sample areas to discuss their experience with domestic violence in that area.

A word is necessary on the interview method with the women's sample. There is little point in approaching the victims of domestic violence with a predetermined schema and a range of deductively derived concepts. Our research started with women's articulation of their experience and general concepts were derived in negotiation with the women themselves. As far as possible, the women were allowed to be the authors of their experiences and particularly in the case of Traveller women their story as it was told directed the method rather than the other way round. This is a process which Liz Kelly (1989) calls building "a cooperative framework" while Dobash and Dobash (1980) describe it as "learning about the problem in its concrete form". In our case this was a time consuming but productive part of the methodology.

Group discussions with women in refuges were used to develop a suitably robust instrument to gather the information as well as to identify issues that were not developed in the literature but which were felt to be important to explore in the Northern Ireland context. These discussions enabled the researchers to find ways to talk to women about their horrific encounters as well as discussing sources of help and suggestions for change.

The resulting semi-structured interview schedule covered what motivated the women to seek help or to make a change; where they went for help – families, friends, voluntary groups, professional agencies; what response they got from anyone they went to for help; any difficulties they experienced in trying to get help; and what suggestions they had for improving support for women. Interviews took approximately two hours to complete. They were recorded and transcribed into both quantitative and qualitative text.

Schedules were also designed for semi-structured interviews with staff in the voluntary and statutory agencies. These interviews covered the level of domestic violence cases encountered; general policy and guidelines for those who deal with domestic violence cases; current practice regarding advice, referrals or other support;

training and amount of expertise in this area of work; liaison with other agencies; difficulties encountered in dealing with domestic violence; and suggestions for changes in agency involvement in domestic violence issues. The design of the two phase approach also enabled professionals to respond to specific issues that were raised by the help-seekers particularly where these related to their own area of work.

Much additional background work was also undertaken. Statistics relating to domestic violence in Northern Ireland were collected from the Northern Ireland Court Service, the Directorate of Information Systems for the DHSS, the R.U.C. and the Northern Ireland Housing Executive. Programmes of study used in the prequalification programmes and in-service education of GPs, health visitors, social workers, nurses, and community workers were analysed, both formally and informally, for the content relating to training and education relevant to domestic violence and relevant interviews were carried out. A marker has to be placed here in that it is not always evident whether or not domestic violence has appeared on the curriculum since it may be subsumed under a different heading as for example in family and child-care programmes. Domestic violence intervention projects in other areas were assessed for their relevance in the context of this research, and an extensive bibliography of existing research on domestic violence was compiled. All these sources and resources have been drawn upon for this study.

Following this introduction, the book has a further five chapters. Chapter Two reviews research literature both in general and with special reference to findings on health and social service professions. Chapter Three reports on women's experiences of domestic violence, using as far as possible their own words and their own accounts of the ways they have responded and the support or lack of it that they received. It makes both harrowing and salutory reading. Chapter Four examines help provision from the point of view of the providers themselves. It juxtaposes for the different groups comments and criticisms on the part of the women with the views – sometimes the very different views – of the providers themselves. Chapter Five treats the voluntary sector in a similar way. Women's

Aid is, of course, the major agency here, but, as we found, there are many other help-providers to whom women from time to time also turn. The major rationale for the project was not research in its own right but research as a prelude to an action initiative. The final chapter, therefore, develops conclusions and recommendations with this in mind.

Two
Literature Review

Research on domestic violence has grown at a very rapid rate in the last decade, faster, some have argued, than in any other substantive area of the social sciences (Gelles and Conte 1990). What we will do in this chapter is to select from this literature to set the context for this Northern Ireland study. First, we will draw attention to the question of the extent of domestic violence, secondly, we will consider the health consequences of domestic violence both for women and for children and thirdly, we will map out the variety of explanatory perspectives available. Finally, we will summarise the current state of understanding of the help-seeking process and the response of the health and social services agencies to domestic violence. This last section most directly reflects the overall concerns of the research project.

The Extent of Domestic Violence

One of the first questions that researchers are often asked is the extent to which the problem of domestic violence occurs. In the United States, a large scale survey, involving over 2000 couples was carried out to address this question in 1975 and again in 1985 (Straus et al 1980, Straus and Gelles 1986). In Britain, no such survey has been undertaken, but the prevalence of domestic violence has been assessed in other ways, using police statistics (Edwards 1986), police and court records (Dobash and Dobash 1979), crime surveys (Worral and Pease 1986) and by specifically focussed local surveys, in Yorkshire (Hanmer and Saunders 1984) and in Hammersmith and Fulham (McGibbon, Cooper and Kelly 1989).

While the victim survey may be thought to provide the most accurate prevalence estimate, this too is likely to lead to an underestimation of the problem. Thus, Kelly and Radford (1991) point out that women are reluctant to admit to being victims either through fear for their safety or as a result of learning to define their experiences as unimportant. Stanko (1985) argues that the prevailing notion that "only bad girls get hurt" means that rather than being exposed as "bad", women stay quiet. Kelly (1988) refers to "forgetting" as a coping strategy and Schechter (1992) found in her interviews that women could not identify with the label "battered" and sought ways to minimise or deny the abuse as a result. For all these reasons, the information which is currently presented from victim surveys and other similar sources should be treated with caution and estimates of prevalence are likely to be underestimates.

Researchers agree, however, that the survey work of Straus and his colleagues provides a useful reference point from which to begin a discussion on prevalency rates. It effectively changed the view that domestic violence was a rare phenomenon. The 1975 survey found that 28 per cent of couples had experienced domestic violence in the previous year and on the basis of such figures, they estimated that over two million American couples had been involved, at some point in their marriage, in what they term a "beating up" incident.

The techniques of this survey, which have been replicated in other countries, have been used to support a proposition of sexual symmetry in domestic violence. However, there is considerable disagreement over the validity of the Conflicts Tactics Scale used by the research team, and particularly over its use to claim that wives are as violent as husbands. The Scale has been criticised for categorising violent acts on a continuum from least to most severe without acknowledging the outcomes for the victim, for treating male and female acts equally and for making no allowance for the power context within which the violence occurs (Dobash, Dobash, Wilson and Daly 1992). Browning and Dutton (1986) show that it leads to differential reporting by husbands and wives, with husbands minimising the violence and ignoring severe injury to their wives or the hospitalization which results from their actions (see also Ptacek 1988; Hoff 1990). Several researchers now stress the importance of adopting a contextually oriented approach to the study of domestic violence. Otherwise the point about who was precipitating the violence and who was reacting to the violence will be lost (Kurz 1989).

Evidence from police and court records (Edwards 1989) and from the British Crime Survey (Worral and Pease 1986) confirms that men are disproportionately the perpetrators and women the victims. The United States National Crime Surveys and the Canadian Urban Victimisation Survey reveal that the number of domestic incidents involving male victims was too low to provide reliable estimates (Johnson 1989). Outside of the Conflict Tactics studies, therefore, the research shows that 95 per cent of all domestic assaults are on women by men with whom they currently live or have previously lived.

In overall terms, taking account of the different methodological strategies for estimating prevalence, studies suggest that from one fifth to one third of all women will be physically assaulted by a partner or ex-partner during their lifetime (Frieze and Browne 1989). In Great Britain, research suggests that violence against women in the home occurs between 1 in 4 and 1 in 10 relationships (McGibbon, Cooper and Kelly 1989).

Forms of Abuse and Their Health Consequences

Homicide figures are frequently used to highlight the seriousness of domestic violence. In Britain, 40 per cent of all female murders are committed by husbands (Edwards 1986). Over half of women murdered in the United States are killed by a current or former male partner (Browne and Williams 1992). In Sweden where it is generally believed that equality between men and women has advanced further in comparison to most other Western industrialised countries, the police statistics for 1989 show that 39 women are battered daily and that one woman is killed every 10 days by a man known to her (Elman and Edwards 1991). Research in the United States shows that women are particularly liable to be killed after they have left the violent relationship and suggests that often women remain in the violent relationship because of the husband's or partner's threats of murder if they leave (Browne 1982, Marzmuk et al. 1992).

Kelly (1988) has suggested that there is a continuum of domestic violence and the Hammersmith and Fulham study confirms this. It shows that the threat of violence is the most common form of abuse and that physical assault is more common than "life threatening" assault involving weapons. Results indicate that:

1 in 3 had been punched or shoved

1 in 5 had been beaten up

1 in 7 had been threatened with death

1 in 7 had been raped by their partner

1 in 10 had been attacked with a weapon.

Mederos (1987) suggests that there is also a continuum of strategies that husbands use to control wives, from anger to emotional abuse to physical violence. What all of these studies point to is the serious nature of domestic violence and its impact on the victims, both physically and psychologically.

The immediate physical impact of domestic violence is well described in the literature (Dobash and Dobash 1979, 1985; Casey 1988; and, for Northern Ireland, Evason 1982). Ruddle and O'Connor (1992) show in the Republic of Ireland that women suffered severe injuries which left their bodies with permanent scars. Some were beaten into unconsciousness and several had to be hospitalised as a result of the violence. In the United States, over 80 per cent of assaults on spouses or ex-spouses result in injuries, compared to 54 per cent of cases of stranger violence (Langley 1991). Moreover, victims of marital violence have the highest rates of internal injuries and unconsciousness and abused women are also more likely to have multiple injuries than accident victims (Burge 1989). All of these findings would suggest that the physical impact of the violence will have implications for the victims well-being in later life. Recent research also suggests an association with delayed physical effects, particularly arthritis, hypertension and heart disease (Council of Scientific Affairs, 1992).

Sexual abuse, rape in marriage and abuse during pregnancy all deserve consideration. Russell (1982), Walker (1985), Frieze (1983) and Kelly (1988) agree that sexual assault is typically associated with battering, with 33 per cent to 46 per cent of abused women reporting it (Frieze and Browne 1989). It is one of the most serious forms of battering, with victims of marital rape suffering many of the same reactions as other rape victims, including very severe depression and suicidal tendencies (Council on Scientific Affairs 1992). Browne (1987) found that women felt particularly threatened and endangered by repeated sexual assault. Feelings of shame and degradation prevent women from talking about this kind of abuse. Moreover, many women do not define forceful sexual assaults as abusive if they are perpetrated by their husbands. Kelly (1988) found suggestions in several women's discussions that abusive men had attempted to make women pregnant without their consent. She notes that forced pregnancy received minimal attention in research and merits further study.

Many women who are victims of domestic violence report that battering is a particularly common occurrence during pregnancy. In a survey of Irish women living in six refuges, Casey (1988) found that out of the 127 women interviewed, 60 per cent had been beaten during their pregnancy. For ten of these women (13 per cent) this resulted in the actual loss of the baby, whilst seventeen (22 per cent) reported the threatened loss of their baby. Evason (1982) also shows that for women in her Northern Ireland study, pregnancy was no defence. American evidence drawn from antenatal clinics, obstetric patients and from a national survey points to between 15 per cent to 17 per cent being assaulted during pregnancy and that 60 per cent of these women experienced recurrent episodes of violence (McFarlane et al 1992; Council on Scientific Affairs 1992; Gelles 1988).

Medical studies show that assaults during pregnancy can result in placental separation, foetal fractures, rupture of the uterus, liver, or spleen and preterm labour (cited in Council on Scientific Affairs, J.A.M.A., 1992). McFarlane et al (1992) also show that abused women are twice as likely as nonabused women to begin antenatal care during the third trimester, which suggests that domestic violence limits women's attendance at antenatal clinics.

The emotional and psychological effects of domestic violence can also have long term consequences for the mental health of a woman. A woman can be held in isolation and forbidden to visit her family, to go out socially or to have personal friends visit the house (Walker 1985; Ruddle and O'Connor 1992). Researchers have compared this experience to that of hostages, with some women exhibiting similar psychological reactions (Graham, Rawlinson and Rimini 1988).

Walker (1979) has described the psychological reactions of women in terms of the "battered woman syndrome", where "learned help-lessness" is an outcome, though not a cause of the violence. It occurs when women become immobilised by fear, preventing them from doing anything to deal with the situation. Kelly (1988) and Schechter (1992) however dispute the view that this is a totally passive reaction. They claim that "learned helplessness" is one way of coping in a situation where women feel that their options are severely limited.

Women who have experienced various forms of abuse report fear, anxiety, depression and withdrawal but it is only recently that researchers have begun to trace this through hospital records. Several studies have found up to 64 per cent of hospitalised female psychiatric patients who had histories of being abused as adults (cited in Warshaw 1989).

Stark and Flitcraft (1979) argue that domestic violence accounts for one in every four suicides attempted by women. Other researchers have found that abused women report more suicide attempts than women who are not abused (Gelles and Straus 1988). In an American hospital emergency sample of 642 women who had been classified as abused, one-sixth had attempted suicide at least once and half more than once (Kurz and Stark, 1988). The researchers argue that the risk of attempted suicide becomes almost five times greater for battered than for nonbattered women. Other findings in relation to mental health are serious somatic disorders such as exaggerated startle response, sleep disturbance, memory impairment and difficulty in concentrating (Douglas 1987).

Nor are the effects of domestic violence confined to women. Stark and Flitcraft (1985), in their review of medical records, found that children whose mothers are battered are more than twice as likely to be physically abused as children whose mothers are not battered. Like Bowker et al. (1988), who also found very high rates of child abuse (70 per cent), they argue that the most important cause and context of child abuse is current abuse of a woman by a man living with her. In the Irish refuges study, 28 per cent of mothers mentioned that their children had been severely beaten by their partners (Casey 1989).

Pagelow (1981) takes the view that a combination of ante- and post-natal emotional and physical abuse suffered by children of abused women often results in a disproportionately high number of these children experiencing handicaps which can be physical, mental or emotional. The literature suggests that children become anxious, insecure and nervous (Casey 1989; Evason 1982). They also have a higher incidence of behaviour problems and lack social competency skills (Jaffe 1986).

Dobash and Dobash (1984) report how children are often burdened with trying to stop the violence or protect their mothers. Studies carried out in refuges show that some children can be distressed initially and often cling to their mothers in the belief that she might disappear (Ruddle and O'Connor 1992). Davies (1991), reporting on an intervention study with male toddlers, suggests that parents, observing the vulnerability expressed in the child's play, belatedly come to recognise that they have misunderstood the impact that witnessing violence has had on the child.

Ruddle and O'Connor (1992) also argue that witnessing domestic violence between parents can have the effect of teaching children that violence is a legitimate response to problems. This is one of the fears, together with concern over the mental health of the children, which prompts many women to leave a violent relationship (Evason 1982).

Explanations of Domestic Violence

The literature on the causes of domestic violence revolves around three main schools of thought. The first concentrates on the pathology of the victim or perpetrator, the second draws on social structural explanations referring to the lack of resources within the family, and the third considers violence between men and women as an agent of overall social relations between the sexes. This last has been referred to as the feminist school of thought, since it takes as its starting point the view that all violence is a reflection of unequal power relationships and that domestic violence reflects the unequal power of men and women, which is reinforced within personal relationships in the family. We discuss each of these briefly and in turn.

Individual Pathology

Within this thinking, either or both partners are described as neurotic or mentally ill – the "mad" or "bad" syndrome. Gayford (1975) suggests in his study that women may have provoked the use of violent behaviour towards them and characterises them into derogatory sterotypes – "Tortured Tina","Go Go Gloria" and "Fanny the Flirt". This "blaming the victim" has been strongly criticised by the main proponents of the other two approaches.

This approach would also, however, take the view that there are certain weaknesses characteristic of men who assault their wives, one of which is susceptibility to alcohol or drug abuse. Bergman and Brismar (1992) in a study of eighteen batterers who had been remanded in custody, lend support to this view. They found that 50 per cent of these men had drunk excessive amounts of alcohol before beating their partners. This is based on a small and unrepresentative sample, however, and it fails to point out that 50 per cent did not use alcohol but were also awaiting sentence for their violent behaviour. As McGregor and Hopkins (1991) argue in the Australian context, valid inferences depend on comparing the rates of violence of alcohol consumers and non-alcohol consumers.

Alcohol abuse can also be used to excuse men's violent assaults. McGregor and Hopkins (1991) argue that drunk men are making choices and can reasonably be held responsible for their behaviour. They take the view that intoxication must not be used as a reason for dealing any more leniently with violent assaults than with drinking and driving. Kaufman et al (1987), and Dobash and Dobash (1992) also argue that alcohol may be more of an excuse for rather than a cause of violence.

Researchers working from other perspectives do not reject alcohol as being a relevant factor. However, they take the view that emphasising alcohol does not provide a sufficient explanation. Careful evaluation of these arguments is particularly relevant in the Northern Ireland context, where, because of a culture which purports to revolve around "drinking", the use of alcohol by individual men has been used frequently as an explanation for their abusive behaviour.

Alcohol apart, another popular theory advanced within this broad approach is that violence is transmitted from one generation to the next, establishing a cycle of violence. According to this theory, people who witness violence or were abused themselves become socialised into seeing violence as a way of life. Others have argued that witnessing violence as a child produces and condones aggressive forms of behaviour in men whilst producing a passive response in women.

Roy's (1982) large scale study of 4,000 American couples found a connection for the abuser but not for the abused. Gelles and Conte (1990), however, found that childhood experience is not the sole determining factor. Reviewing research in the 1980s, they argue that the process by which violence is transferred from one generation to the next is more complex than simple modeling of behaviour. Stark and Flitcraft (1985) also point out that many who have been abused as children do not become abusers. Smith (1989) concludes that the explanatory power of the cycle of violence thesis must be seen as only partial and advises that it should be treated in the same way as excessive use of alcohol – as a contributing factor but not as a sole, direct or primary cause.

Social Structural Explanations

This theoretical approach emphasises domestic violence as a response to social structural factors. It argues that stress in the family results from a lack of resources (low income and bad housing for example) and can precipitate violence. Harris and Bologh (1985) argue that violence can enable working class men for example to compensate for their low status jobs. Middle class men who perceive a threat to their status of the "successful breadwinner" may also respond by using violence.

This theory is also used to explain why women return to abusive relationships. Thus, an abused woman with few resources or access to employment may perceive her alternatives inside the marriage as being more rewarding and less costly than alternatives outside. In such cases the woman's economic needs take precedence over her physical and emotional needs to be free from abuse. Johnson (1992) uses this approach in her study of 426 abused women who sought help from a refuge. She found that women are likely to return home to the abuser when the annual household income is high, when they are unemployed, and when they have negative perceptions of themselves. Rather than the individual's psychopathology being analysed, this approach shows that the woman's decision-making process about leaving or returning is a complex one involving economic and social factors. Moreover, it shifts the problem from being a personal one to being a public one.

Unequal Power Relationships

This perspective views domestic violence as a reflection of the wider unequal power relationship of men and women in society. It is used to explain both the personal violence of men towards women and children as well as the process by which the woman becomes victimised in attempting to seek help for herself or her children. This has provided the most expansive area of the literature in the '80s and is an approach adopted by sociologists (Pagelow 1981; Pahl 1985; Dobash and Dobash 1979, 1992; Hanmer and Maynard 1987; Yllo and Bograd 1988; Kelly 1988; Edwards 1988), psychologists (Walker 1984) and medical practitioners (Flitcraft 1992).

Dobash and Dobash (1992) provide both an historical and contemporary analysis showing how in patriarchal society, men's use of violence as a form of control over women is maintained and endorsed by legal, political and economic institutions. Historically, women have been confined to the home and excluded from positions of power and status outside the family. Whilst structural aspects have prevented women from changing or influencing the social order, it has been patriarchal ideology which has rationalised and legitimised the subordinate position of women. In other words the socialisation process has ensured the acceptance of that order by both men and women.

In their research work, Dobash and Dobash adopt the "context-specific" approach to show how husbands have sought and still seek to control their wives by violence. At the core of this is a concrete analysis of the violence and its immediate contexts, for example the acts, motives and interpretations of those who perpetrate and those who experience violence. They link this with gender specific cultural beliefs, socialisation and practices. In such an approach, motives such as jealousy, sexual problems, alcohol abuse or childhood exposure to violence might become the contributory factors to an abusive situation, but can only be explained if they are placed in the overall context of men's use of violence to dominate and control women in intimate relationships. Violence can be condoned or sanctioned by a set of cultural beliefs which upholds the sanctity of marriage or women's economic dependancy on men. Ruddle and O'Connor (1992) found that for Irish women, their central identity was tied into being married – even at the cost of violence. McKibbon, Cooper and Kelly (1989) also make the point that for some ethnic minority women, their status without a husband is important since leaving a violent marriage can result in exclusion from the community.

Levinson (1989) lends support to to this approach. In a study of 90 societies, he found that male decision making power in the family and restrictions on women to divorce were strong predictors of domestic violence. Although Yllo (1988) found something similar in her study of American states, she notes that wife abuse did not simply decline as women's status improved. Domestic violence also increased in those states in which women's status was highest relative to men's. Yllo believes that this may be an indicator that rapid change towards equality could bring a violent backlash by husbands.

In summary, the literature on domestic violence seems to have shifted from the pathological to the more radical approaches of studying the victimisation process. In their more recent work, Dobash and Dobash (1992) show how the response by individual agencies is influenced by their overall approach to domestic violence. In the U.S.A. for example the therapeutic response to women seeking help was strongly influenced by the pathological approach. Alternatively in Britain, the government has acted more in terms of a social

structural approach by developing a statutory response to the problem. The need for public sector housing, adequate social security
benefits and increased refuge provision has also been central to the
British analysis which sees these as a means of reducing the unequal
power relationship between men and women. This brings us directly
to the final section in which we will review some of the responses by
health and social service agencies to women who have experienced
domestic violence.

The Help-Seeking Process

Dobash and Dobash (1985) show that most women do seek assistance at some point in the abusive relationship. Binney et al (1981)
found that only 1 per cent of women had told no-one about the
violence. Studies have shown that almost all women turn at first to
family and friends and only as the violence increases do they seek
help from more formal agencies while continuing to use family
networks (Dobash and Dobash 1985; Pahl 1985).

Beyond this, however, studies vary on the extent to which contacts
with agencies are clearly reported. In the Republic of Ireland, Ruddle
and O'Connor (1992) found that whilst 50 per cent of the women
living in refuges had contacted social workers only 20 per cent had
consulted a General Practioner. Evason (1982) on the other hand
found in her Northern Ireland study, that a much smaller proportion (18 per cent) had contacted social workers whilst 50 per cent
had sought assistance from a GP. The list below gives some indication of the proportions using different agencies in Great Britain:

Police	60%+
GPs	52%-80%
Social Services	54%-75%
Housing Departments	30%+
Others	Less than 30%

(Sources: Dobash and Dobash 1979; Hanmer et al. 1989; Edwards 1989; Bourlet 1990).

While these figures show that the police are the most frequently
contacted agency, what research is available in Northern Ireland
suggests that women may experience unique problems in obtaining

help from the police (Evason 1982; Montgomery and Bell 1986). Montgomery (1991) suggests that the political conflict has impacted on police procedures and practices in such a way that it raises the question as to whether other agencies are contacted instead by women seeking help.

What of the agencies' responses to the help-seeker? There is general agreement that both statutory and voluntary agencies are in a position to help women in abusive relationships, but the research also indicates that they may fail to identify or may redefine the problem in a number of ways. Evidence for this is set out below, together with an enumeration of some of the main reasons researchers have considered for it, namely their professional orientations, their lack of knowledge and training and their attitudes and beliefs. Available research focuses in the main on the medical profession, but material on health visitors and social workers is included wherever possible.

a) *Failure to Identify Domestic Violence*

A number of studies have shown that doctors often fail to identify abuse when signs and symptoms are present. In one study, carried out in an accident and emergency department, doctors identified one in 35 of their female patients as battered while a review of the medical charts indicated that one in four were likely to have been battered (Kurz and Stark 1988). Warshaw (1989) found that doctors' discharge notes correctly indicated domestic violence in only 8 per cent of the cases in which explicit information about abuse (such as patient statements) or very strong indications of abuse were recorded in the medical charts. Randall (1990) estimates that between 22 per cent and 35 per cent of women presenting with complaints to emergency departments are suffering from injuries or symptoms related to on-going abuse. Borkowski (1983) cites a British study which revealed a monthly average of only two recorded cases in the accident and emergency departments of two large general hospitals. Stark et al. (1979) analysed the medical records of 481 women in a one month period in a major hospital's casualty department and showed that the number of abused women using the service was as much as ten times higher than that estimated by doctors.

Failure to identify can occur repeatedly. Stark et al. (1979) found that 23 per cent of abused women had brought six to 10 abuse-related injuries to the attention of clinicians. They noted that approximately one in five abused women presenting to doctors had sought medical attention 11 times previously for domestic related assaults. These researchers argue that when doctors do not identify abuse, it is most likely to continue and will often escalate.

When a diagnosis of abuse is missed, treatment is likely to be inappropriate and potentially harmful. For example, Stark et al. (1979) point out that doctors often prescribe medications for abused women, usually for pain relief or mild tranquilisers. These prescriptions are contraindicated because the abuse victims are at an increased risk of suicide and drug or alcohol abuse and such drugs may limit the victim's alertness or hamper the decision-making process, in turn leaving the victim more vulnerable to assault (Dobash, Dobash and Cavanagh 1985).

Smith (1989) notes that since some women are deterred, or prevented, from visiting their GPs by threats of further violence then health visitors and midwives have a role to play. Their home visits could help to identify the problem by offering an opportunity for women to talk and seek and receive help. Stark and Flitcraft (1988) claim however that because of patriarchal medical ideologies and practices, these health professionals as well as medical practitioners fail to recognise battering and instead treat women as having psychological problems. They argue that failing to diagnose abuse may further the victim's sense of entrapment and thereby contribute to victimisation. Pagelow (1981) and Hanmer and Maynard (1985) also show that the experience of ineffectual responses keeps women with violent partners and leads them to believe that nothing they do can bring about a solution to their problems.

Why should diagnosis be missed? Studies have shown that doctors are reluctant to raise the subject with patients who show signs of potential abuse and do not ask in-depth questions about how victims were injured (Dobash and Dobash 1979; Warshaw 1989). The fear of offending the patient by not wanting to overstep the bounds of what is private and yet acknowledging that domestic violence has medical consequences can leave professionals in a dilemma (Sugg and Inui 1992). The women too may be reluctant to raise the problem. Gin et al. (1990) show that in a study of out-patient departments, more women had had experience of domestic violence than felt able to discuss the problem with the doctor. In Dobash and Dobash's (1979) study, 80 per cent of women victims were examined by doctors but only a quarter of the women reported that they had been beaten. However, evidence suggests that abused women expect doctors to initiate the discussions, that they favour inquiries about physical and sexual abuse and that they will respond to questions if they are asked directly in a sympathetic and non-judgemental way (Friedman et al. 1992).

Time is a further factor. Sugg and Inui (1992) refer to domestic violence as a "Pandora's box" – with doctors describing it is as one more issue that will consume their scarce time. As in other studies, professionals make comments about domestic violence being such a rare event that it is not a good investment of time (Dobash, Dobash and Cavanagh 1985, McGibbon et al 1989). Accident and Emergency staff in Britain have also been shown to have little time available for initiating the longer-term management of the emotional sequelae of violence. Shepherd (1990) found that staff had not referred victims to hospital social workers. He believes that not taking the time to follow through has long term implications for the victims making it more difficult for them to cope with the assault.

Not surprisingly, perhaps, in the light of all this, the literature also emphasises the extent to which professionals under-estimate the number of cases in their existing case loads where domestic violence is a factor. Estimates made by social workers (Maynard 1985) and by the medical and health professions (Borkowski et al. 1983) contrast with the reported contacts in victim studies. Maynard (1985) found domestic violence hidden under some other classification in the social work case records which she analysed. In marked contrast to the advice from social workers that she would only find one or two cases, she estimated that domestic violence was involved in about one-third of the cases.

All this indicates a mismatch between problem and response. In a survey that asked 1,000 abused women to rate the effectiveness of various professionals in addressing domestic violence, health care professionals had the lowest rating, ranking behind refuges, solicitors, social workers, police and clergy (Bowker and Maurer 1987).

b)   *Redefining the Problem*

A number of studies have found that professionals will deal with issues from the standpoint of their own professional orientation and seem reluctant to accept a more widely defined role (Binney et al. 1981; Maynard 1985; Dobash, Dobash and Cavanagh 1985). Warshaw (1989), for example, notes in her study of casualty departments that the doctor-patient interaction tended to obscure rather than elucidate information about abuse. She claims "medicine's epistemologic model of care reconstructs abusive relationships through a medical encounter in which what is most significant is not seen. Nurses are less affected by the model but are under institutional constraints that lead to similar outcomes". Shepard (1991), focussing on social workers, argues that they lack practice models that emphasise socio-cultural factors and focus instead on internal psychological processes and the interactional dynamics of the relationship.

Orr (1984) suggests different but no less problematic responses of professionals at each stage. Early on, those who have suffered repeated physical injuries and minor medical/mental complaints are treated as solely a medical problem. Professionals treat the injuries and symptoms of abuse, rather than addressing the on-going family violence which is at the root of their victim's health problems (American Medical Association 1992). Later, those presenting with more psychosocial problems meet with a psychiatric referral. This again can ignore the root of the problem and in itself can attach a stigma to the problem of domestic violence. When women reach the third stage, they present with severe medical or mental health problems and frequently have made multiple suicide attempts. Problems arise at this third stage not only because the abuse can turn to self abuse but because the help-providers see the symptoms as the cause of the abuse rather than the consequence. Gelles and Harrop (1989) argue that mental health professionals must learn to treat the psychological consequences of abuse and not confuse these with the precursors of the abuse. Orr (1984) believes also that the

approach taken by health professionals can also reinforce traditional female stereotyping where, for example, putting on make-up
and doing housework are seen as signs of recovery – the price to be
paid for being cured.

Social service staff also redefine the problem. Since domestic violence is not a statutory responsibility for the social services, concern
usually focuses on issues about children and child welfare (Maynard
1985; McGibbon at al. 1989). Orr (1984) also finds that health
visitors may adopt this strategy, viewing the family as the key unit,
with the needs of children as paramount and other members' needs
as subservient. There are real dilemmas for women in this child-
centred approach. Maguire (1988) comments on the cases of women
who have left home and are residing in poor accommodation who
are then informed by social workers that they must find suitable
housing or their children will be taken into care. These researchers
also note that the fear of having their children placed in care often
prevents women from making contacts with professionals in the
first place.

c)   *Wider Issues*

Two further problems have been identified as lack of knowledge and
training, and the use of traditional attitudes and beliefs. Professionals' lack of knowledge about sources of help may account for the low
levels of practical assistance reported by victims (Dobash and Dobash
1985; Evason 1982; Sugg and Inui 1992). McGibbon et al. (1989)
found in social services in Hammersmith and Fulham that much of
the practical advice given to women was limited and that the onus
for change was often placed on the women themselves. Some social
workers felt it was appropriate to talk to the abusive men but such
involvement was most frequently discussed in terms of "family
therapy", which they interpreted as working with the couple to
reconstruct the relationship.

Smith (1989) comments that the emphasis on inter-personal skills
in social work training should enable social workers to intervene
effectively at an early stage, particularly if the assailant shows some
remorse and is willing to participate in counselling. In practice

however action comes too late. Only when the violence has grown very severe does it seem that any response is forthcoming. By then efforts to reconcile the partners may not only be fruitless but also inappropriate, since they risk putting the woman's life in danger (Smith 1989; Dobash and Dobash 1992).

McIlwaine (1989) argues that doctors, and other professionals, should be well informed about sources of help such as Women's Aid and be prepared to refer women to other agencies. In her article in the British Medical Journal, she notes that students should be taught about the scale, form and consequences of domestic violence but that no information is available about whether such teaching is available in the undergraduate programmes of British medical schools.

In the Hammersmith and Fulham study, McGibbon et al. (1989) also found a tendency amongst social workers to use what they describe as "common-sense" individualistic explanations when discussing both the causes of and responses to domestic violence. Shepard (1991) also notes that although social workers encounter domestic violence in a variety of settings such as child protection, mental heath and sub-stance dependance, they frequently disagree about the nature and cause of the violence. As a result of this disagreement, domestic violence becomes a controversial area of work. Flitcraft (1992) argues that although there has been a profound change in the public response to domestic violence over the past 15 years, informal social norms and stereotyped gender roles still legitimate control of one partner over the other. These, in turn, allow professionals to ration-alise abuse in adult relationships. She comments that in an American study of general practitioners' attitudes about domestic violence the doctors strategies – denial, minimisation, and rationalisation – echo the voices of the abuser who neither identifies nor accepts responsi-bility for his violent behaviour.

Traditional attitudes regarding women's roles as wives and mothers and stereotypes about why violence occurs may result in victim blaming (Maynard 1985). The help-providers may perceive that the woman is the problem if she does not act on their advice to end the relationship, go to a refuge or get an exclusion order. Schechter (1982) shows that ending victimisation can be a lengthy process, especially where there are few options. She points out that women continually assess the situation and make choices. In view of the lack of resources and social supports for leaving, staying in an abusive relationship should not be interpreted as acceptance of violence. Leaving does not always end the violence either – for 50 per cent of women, it means them being followed and further attacked (Browne 1987). It should be noted however that women do leave their violent partners, thus contradicting professionals' views of women as passive victims (Kelly 1988).

Professionals may also engage in labelling. Kurz and Stark (1988) found that doctors labelled patients as neurotic, hysterical, "a crock" and "a hypochondriac" significantly more frequently when it was known that the person was at risk for abuse than not. Kurz (1987) has documented how individual staff in emergency departments label battered women as social cases rather than defining them as true medical ones. Staff felt that they made extra trouble and work for doctors. Battered women who did not look like typical victims were frequently not recognised as battered. They were sent home without paying attention to their situation. This study also documents how after training in how to respond to domestic violence, the accident and emergency staff had a higher rate of recognition and intervention with battered women.

This review of the literature suggests that far from domestic violence being a rare occurrence, it is frequently a regular and repeated event in the lives of a sizeable proportion of women. Estimates vary from between one in ten to one in four women and point to the need for professionals to be more alert to both identifying and responding to it. Research on the impact of domestic violence also confirms its serious and long-term consequences – both for the women and for their children. It can have particularly serious outcomes for pregnant women. More recently, research has begun to focus on the social, economic and cultural factors rather than on the individual pathological factors in attempting to explain the cause of domestic violence. Attempts to develop a model which addresses patriarchy and which reflects unequal power and the control which is asserted over women in violent relationships are significant and are a major focus of British and Irish research in this field. Despite these shifts however, it appears that the response of the health and social service agencies is still inhibited by a range of factors. These may be broadly categorised as professional orientation; adherence to narrowly defined professional roles; lack of knowledge about sources of help and about the dynamics of domestic violence; lack of identification of the problem and misplaced beliefs, attitudes and stereotypes.

THREE

Women's Experiences of Domestic Violence

The serious and extensive nature of the problem of domestic violence has been clearly illustrated in the literature review. We now turn to the facts of violence against women in the home in Northern Ireland. This chapter, based on extracts from the interviews with women who suffered the abuse, provides a vivid picture of the nature of domestic violence, and confirms that domestic violence has serious consequences for the well-being of both women and children. The women's stories also give us an understanding of their reactions to the violence, their decision making process, and the particular constraints placed on their actions. As a result of the traditional attitudes toward marriage and the family in Northern Ireland and the difficulties in getting help, the reaction for many women has been to keep violence hidden in the home.

The chapter also uses women's descriptions of the violence to challenge some of the standard explanations of domestic violence as discussed in the literature review and to argue that a recognition of the inequality of power between men and women within the family and in the wider society is essential in any discussion of the causes of domestic violence. The impact of the political situation in Northern Ireland on the help-seeking process of women is also discussed in this section. In addition, there is a consideration of the particular needs of special groups such as Traveller and Asian women, and women living in rural areas. Women's advice and suggestions on what should be done about domestic violence forms the conclusion to the chapter.

A brief note is necessary on the characteristics of the 56 women who formed the sample. Twenty-two women were living in a refuge at the time of the interview, while 28 had already ended their relationships and were living on their own in the former marital home or in new housing. Six women were still living with their partners. The majority (45) were or had been married, while 11 were cohabiting. Ages ranged from 18 to 52 years, but the largest group (43 per cent) were between 30 and 40 years. The sample included 31 women from the Catholic community, 22 from the Protestant community, and 3 from the Travelling community. Based on information about the women's and partners' occupations, the majority (41) was assessed to be from working class house-holds. The sample included ten women from middle class or professional households, three Traveller women and two from farming families. The women came from a wide distribution of areas throughout Northern Ireland (see Table 1, Annex 2). Most came from urban areas, with the largest single group being from West Belfast, and six women in all from rural areas.

Nature and Impact of the Violence

Women's descriptions of the violence against them showed that it began early in their relationships and increased in intensity and frequency; that it was ongoing, rather than isolated incidents; and that it was serious, often requiring medical treatment. Women were beaten while they were pregnant, some were raped, and many took overdoses because of the violence.

Three-quarters of the women said violence started very early in their relationships (Table 2, Annex 2), with 32 women (57 per cent) saying that they had been hit by the end of the first year. These included two women who were first beaten on their wedding night. Only two were hit before they married. Three women indicated that the violence began during their first pregnancy or after the birth of their first child. For most in our survey, violence was a fact of life for the duration of the relationship, ending only with the end of the relationship through separation or death. There was a small group of six women in our survey who were still living with the abusive partner, trying to make the relationship work in spite of the violence. The largest group of women (19) stayed in the violent relationships up to five years (Table 3, Annex 2). Another 15 stayed for up to 10 years. However 12 women (21 per cent) were in their relationships for over ten years, and eight endured the violence for over 16 years.

What kind of injuries were involved? Here is one account:

> He trailed me round the house. We had these, you know, drawers and
> wardrobes that had brass handles on them and he just trailed me by the hair,
> banged my head off everything. At this stage I was about three or four
> months pregnant. And he'd kicked me up and down the stairs and trailed me
> through the kitchen, and through the living room, used my head to open the
> doors and all. You know, just banged it off the doors. And he brought a
> Stanley knife and he said, 'If you ever do that (go to the police) again I'll
> mark you for life.'

This is but one example of the full horror of the violence encountered and the fear and dread felt by the women. Some of the injuries
resulting from the violence are listed in the accompanying box. We
did not specifically ask about all injuries, but only those considered
to be the 'worst incident', or those which required hospital care. It
was evident in the interviews that there were other serious injuries
and some were too painful to discuss.

Injuries Reported

permanent eye damage	broken nose (2)	split head
broken ribs (2)	broken jaw (2)	prolapsed womb
head butted	fractured skull	ruptured eardrum
punched in head	cracked ribs	rape (5)
choked	knocked unconscious	attempted rape
broken teeth	stitches in mouth	miscarriage (2)
dislocated nose	broken finger	premature birth
head injury	black eye	split mouth
bruising		

Over half of the women (30) said they needed medical treatment for
their injuries, while 22 women (39 per cent) required hospital
treatment at least once. One third, 19 women, were hit while they
were pregnant and two women suffered miscarriages. One woman
said "I buried a baby because of him". Men took advantage of women's
pregnancy to cause more pain as one woman described, "during my
third pregnancy, he [i.e. the baby] was lying on a nerve on my leg, and I
couldn't walk, and he used to kick me on the leg, you know, because he
knew it was sore."

Five women told us they were raped, another spoke of an attempted rape. Several women told us that they had sex when they didn't want to and others had given in just to please their partner. The presence of children did not stop this abuse. *"My wee boy, he was crammed up against the wall. My husband was getting very very abusive, and holding me down on the bed and the wee boy was screaming and roaring".*

Marital rape was one of the problems that women were most reluctant to disclose. Agencies such as the Rape Crisis Centre have found similar reluctance in practice with women in Northern Ireland. We often found that women told about the rapes with great difficulty or included this point almost as an afterthought. *"I used to let him have his way with me before he went to the pub to try and stop him from going to the pub. But he would go to the pub anyway and then he would have his way with me anyway after he came from the pub. Ach, I suppose you could say that he raped me. That's very hard to admit."*

There were some women who attempted self-harm. Eight women took overdoses as a result of the violence; one did this four times. One woman told about her daughter who was beaten and raped by her partner. *"He [the partner] said that would be nothing to what she [i.e. the daughter] would get when he come home. So her only way out then, she thought, was to take an overdose."*

Men used a variety of weapons as they attacked their partners. Several of the women were threatened with guns. One woman whose husband didn't have a gun in the house told her several times he knew where he could get one to use on her. But the men used a variety of other more 'ordinary' weapons including an ashtray, pram, guitar, frying pan, camogie stick, baseball bat, butcher's knife, bread knife, radio.

It was both mental and physical. You know, I am just thinking of times when he would put the gun to my head, and play Russian Roulette with it, with me. . . . but there was no physical harm done then."

He beat me first and kicked me until I was down on the ground and when I was lying there he went in and put on the steel toecapped boots that he wore for work and came back out and started into me again. Kicked me about the stomach and down below when I was pregnant.

Threats of more violence sometimes had an even greater impact on the women than the violence itself. Several women reported that they stayed longer in the violent relationship because of this fear.

> *He said if I ever went – he would kill me – if I ever contacted a solicitor. I was really scared. I think he would kill me.*
>
> *I thought he was going to kill me that night. He was like in a sing-song voice: 'Come on – see what I've got for you. I've got a big knife waiting for you – come on till you see what you're going to get.'*

Impact of Violence on Children

After her daughter died from an overdose three days after her 18th birthday, a grief stricken mother thought it was *"through the violence of her father, the marriage – she was always the one that took it the worst. She was always the one to rescue me."* Though this was the most tragic case, this research has found that homes where men were violent to their wives often became dangerous places for their children as well.

Similar to the findings of other research (Casey 1989; Evason 1982), there were many children in this survey who have been emotionally and physically scarred by the violent attacks on their mothers (see list). Some of the children exhibited symptoms such as nightmares only as long as the violent relationship lasted. For other children, the effects were seen for a short time after the family had broken up. But some mothers told us about very long term effects on children, like one young man who, now in his twenties, still stammers in his father's presence.

Impact of Domestic Violence on Children	
died from overdose	witnessed violence
heard the violence	took overdose
taken out of bed to watch beating	abused, beaten
hit father, then beaten	reject, despise father
still afraid	afraid of hitting girls
withdrawn, quiet	won't leave mother
suggested leaving	protective of mother
scared out of their wits	personalities affected
teenage daughters afraid of men	school work affected
afraid of losing mother	nightmares
children in care, mother can't cope	stammers in father's presence

'Don't Hit My Mummy!', a slogan currently used in the Women's Aid community aware-ness poster campaign, does sum up many of the stories told by the women. One nine year old saved her mother's life. When her husband came at her with a bread knife, *"my door opened and she was screaming: 'You leave my mommy alone, don't you do that!' I wouldn't be here now cause he would have killed me that night."* But too often the child's protectiveness brought violent abuse on the child as well as the mother. And several of the fathers began by abusing their wives, but then turned on the children as well.

We found that mothers often belatedly recognised the impact of the violence on their children (cf Davies 1992). Several mothers told us that it was only after leaving the relationship, some years later, that they realised that their children were affected by the violence. One woman thought she had protected the children from the violence, *"But they are telling me now, what a lot of the violence they had seen, and it's affected them. I would try and placate him until I got them up to bed, and then whenever I would come down, he would start, and it's only now that they are telling me about sneaking downstairs, and how they seen him hitting me with a frying pan, or trying to cut my throat with a butcher's knife."* Mothers have also learned that children's own sense of security was threatened by the violence. Years after the violence occurred, mothers found teenage children still terrified that there would be some reason for them to be separated from their mother.

Women's awareness of the effect on their children and their ability to protect them was often impaired because they were so wrapped up in their own problems brought on by the violence. One woman now recognises that *"I was more worried about myself actually. But obviously if it affected me, it affected the children."*

Social workers we interviewed were concerned that concentration on the issue of domestic violence might turn the abused women into 'man haters'. We found, however, that the violence by fathers was already having this effect on some children. Numbers of children rejected and despised their fathers. Young children were afraid to go near them. And several teenage daughters had serious difficulty relating to men. One woman felt her 16 year old daughter was badly affected. *"I know she doesn't trust them (men) or can't stand them. If she goes out and if they look at her, she comes into the house crying".*

There has been much research on the possibility of inter-generational transmission of violence which argues that children will accept violence as a legitimate response because of their experiences at home. Several of the women in our study were afraid this would happen and left relationships because of these fears. *"I feel that if I had stayed there, he would have grown up like his father, because he wouldn't have known any different, and I didn't want him to turn out like that."* However, other women found not a tolerance for but a rejection of violence by their male children and the adoption of a protective attitude toward women. One woman described how her young son refused to fight back when girls hit him while playing on the street. *"No, no, no, I wouldn't hit a woman', he says."*

The interviews showed there were contradictory responses by help-providers to the domestic violence. Some women said they themselves had been blamed because of the dangers posed to their children by the violence. However the responses of statutory agencies described by the women were often to ignore or minimise the violence, appearing to give legitimation to the use of violence by the male partner. For example, several women in this study lost custody of all or some of their children. Courts and social workers did not seem to consider the history of violence to be relevant in the consideration of these men to be fit fathers. When one woman raised this issue with her social worker, the violence was called an 'isolated incident.' Other women found social workers making judgments against them because they were in a refuge, while their husbands were "living in a nice home."

Several women were unhappy with the lack of social worker response to the needs of children who were affected by the violence. None of the women were offered any sort of support, such as counselling, for their children and those who asked for support found interest only if the children were physically hurt. Children who lived for a period of time in a Women's Aid refuge have had the opportunity for support. Provision of a childcare worker in each refuge enables the children to talk about what happened and get more help if needed. In addition, children in families who had a referral to a family centre for therapeutic support had access to long term professional help. But these centres are limited to caring for very small numbers. Other children and women had to cope on their own and it was these women who most frequently mentioned the need for some type of counselling and childcare provision.

Explanations of Domestic Violence

While it is often claimed that alcohol abuse is a major contributory factor to domestic violence, Chapter Two suggested that there is little conclusive evidence of a causative relationship between the two. The following was the pattern of responses reported by the women in our sample:

	No.	%
Partner hit when drunk and sober	25	45
Partner hit when drunk	12	21
Partner did not drink	11	20
No answer	8	14
Total	56	100

Alcohol abuse was a relevant factor in a majority (66 per cent) of the relationships. However, in only a minority of cases (21 per cent) was the woman hit only when her partner drank, and 20 per cent of the abused women said their partners did not drink. However over two-thirds (67 per cent) of the 37 respondents who cited alcohol as a factor said they were also hit when their partner had not been drinking.

For those women who were hit by partners when either drunk or sober, the drinking served as a predictor of violence for them. They knew to expect violence when their partner was drinking. However they were also hit when the partner had a hangover or in between drinking bouts. For some, the violence initially related only to drinking, but over time it had extended so that eventually there was no difference in the pattern of violence between drunk or sober times.

Some of the 12 women whose partners' violence was solely linked to alcohol saw distinct differences in personality and behaviour between the drunk and sober periods. "*My husband is an alcoholic, but*

*at the same time he is a good man. He loves me and our child to bits. It's
this illness that he has."* Many of these women did attempt to get help
from AA or alcohol abuse units. But others thought men should still
be responsible for their actions. *"If he knew he was going to be violent,
he shouldn't've took that drink."*

The women's stories gave much more support to the view that men
use violence to control their wives' or partners' behaviour. In their
descriptions of physical and emotional abuse, the women told of the
many ways in which their partners, both married and cohabiting,
had dominated or controlled their lives (see list).

Women's Descriptions of Emotional Abuse and Control

he put me down	I was brainwashed
I felt good for nothing	he was jealous
he always had to have the upper hand	he was possessive
he disagreed with anything I said	he was domineering
he alienated friends and family	he was powerful
I was not allowed to work	he was terrifying
he controlled my movements	I had to obey
he treated house and me as his possessions	he picked my clothes
he followed me everywhere	I was kept a prisoner

The descriptions illustrate a number of aspects of emotional abuse
which men used to control their partners. Some men restricted
women's movements and choice of company, leaving them totally
isolated. Many women were totally cut off from family and friends,
some were not even allowed to visit their mothers. Some are finding
it very hard to adjust now that they are on their own, because of the
years of isolation when they couldn't have any friends.

As well as the severence of social networks, the women experienced
a process of what many called brainwashing or thought control.
One said, *"It was as if I didn't have a personality. He had sort of
brainwashed me as if I was hopeless and nobody else would want me.
Your brain takes that in and you start believing that. I honestly think that
men who batter they do condition their wives to what they want them to
be."* The brainwashing included convincing the women that they
were never right, that they would not be able to cope alone and that
they were 'no good'.

Male traditional attitudes towards women's role in the home prompted much violence. One woman said that early in the marriage she realised that, "*If I stepped over a certain line outside these parameters of behaviour, he could be violent.*" Women who challenged these patriarchal male attitudes by going to work or gaining education met with abuse. One woman said that the violence started when she started working as a secretary for a community organisation. "*He didn't want me to work. I should be at home looking after the children – that's what his mummy had always done.*" For some women it was too much and they gave it up. "*I worked in a factory, but it got that much that I couldn't take it any more, because he was actually thinking when I was working overtime, that I was away with a man. He came up to the factory and followed the taxi down home.*" Another found things got worse when she went back to university. "*That was stepping outside the bounds.*" She felt her husband, a teacher, thought he was the only one that was allowed to have knowledge or to be educated.

Though only a minority of the women in our sample were in regular employment, it was an ordeal for them to keep their jobs because of the attitudes and violence of their partners. One woman's business was destroyed and other women told of being followed to work regularly. One man regularly rang his partner at work or came looking for her. Fortunately she had a very sympathetic employer. Another had to make sure no one from work found out what was happening to her because her reputation as an experienced employee would have been damaged. These limitations on women either at work or in education fit the pattern whereby men are attempting to keep women dependent and in the home. For all, the deprivation of access to social networks for support and to independent means of gaining their own income made it more difficult for women to leave the relationship and live on their own.

For the women in the survey, getting over the emotional abuse and the 'brainwashing' was one of the most difficult tasks on the road to leading independent lives. Support was necessary to overcome the emotional dependency, to regain confidence and to make their own decisions. As one woman described, "*I was a non person. I was an extension of him. He told me what to do, and I would follow the rules, just so I could have a quieter life. That was then, I've changed now.*"

Women's Reaction to Violence

During the early stages of the violence women either did nothing or looked to their wider families for support. Families were the main source of support in the early and later stages of the relationships, while women placed greater reliance on professional support agencies at times of severe crises.

Women's own family, and particularly female family members, were the first point of contact for telling about the violence or seeking support for two-thirds (37) of the women (see Table 4, Annex 2). Mothers were most often the person first contacted. Ten women went to a variety of statutory and voluntary agencies, while six women talked to other informal sources, which included partners' families and their own friends and neighbours.

When the women were asked what they did after the first, worst and last incidents of violence, most replied that they had told no-one the first time violence occurred, but ten women did talk to someone in their family (see Table 5, Annex 2). Of the 48 women who told us about their worst experience, the largest single response was still nothing. But the severity of the violence on these occasions and the crisis point that had been reached is clearly indicated by the number of contacts made with professional agencies – hospitals and police in particular. The family was reduced in importance as a point of contact, with only five women going to them first. Several women who had gone to their families for help during the early stage of violence, stopped doing so because of fears for their safety, as partners often either attacked or threatened families who 'interfered'.

The overwhelming response to the 'last time' violence occurred for our respondents was to leave their home. Forty out of the 56 women (71 per cent) left then (see Table 5). Only three women still did nothing about the violence. This question was not applicable to 3 women in our sample because their partner was no longer violent. For those women who did not leave the home, contact with the police and solicitors was the most frequent response.

An examination of the first point of contact made by women when they were leaving, again shows a heavy reliance on family support.

Fourteen out of the 40 women who left went to their families first (see Table 6, Annex 2). The next most usual point of contact was the Housing Executive and social work agencies, followed by the police. Only four women, all of whom had previously stayed in a refuge, went directly to a refuge.

In spite of the fact that so many women reported that they did nothing in the early stages of violence, it would be mistaken to view the women as simply passive victims. The women adopted many different methods to cope with or stop the violence, whilst continuing to try to make a success of the relationship. Several women fought back either verbally or physically, at least in the early stages of the violence, but most found that that only made the violence worse. Only two succeeded in stopping the violence. One of these had army training and said, *"As soon as I turned on him, he stopped. A bully stops."* But because she proved she could defend herself, when she went to court the magistrate refused to recognise that hers was a case of domestic violence.

When asked how they coped with the violence, the largest response from women was *"I gave in and did whatever he wanted."* Women found ways to placate their partners with sexual favours, nice meals, money; they went out of their way to avoid arguments. Another set of responses centred around communication, either by talking to their partners in an attempt to reason with them and calm then down or by ending communication – giving them the 'silent treatment'. Smaller numbers of the women said they left the house, 'lived on their nerves', or handled it themselves, and 'got used to it'.

The interviews indicated that another method used by women to cope was to deny or minimise the violence as one woman did when she described how *"he busted my ear drum once, and I couldn't wash my hair for weeks." "Now"*, she says, *"I have a slight hearing problem, but not too bad."* Walker (1979) and others have written of women's responses such as these in domestic violence situations as a process of "learned helplessness", referring to women's lack of reactions to repeated abuse. However, others (Stanko 1985) argue that this is not a totally passive reaction. Learned helplessness may be an important method of maintaining sanity in a situation where a person feels their options to be very severely limited.

Leaving a Violent Partner

Making the decision to leave or end the relationship was, for most, a long and difficult process, one to be adopted only as a last resort. In the experience of Women's Aid, women generally make many attempts to get out of the situation before finally ending their relationships. During 1991 to 1992, 56 per cent of the women who came to Women's Aid refuges returned to the marital home. The decisions women made were usually based on a rational appraisal of the limitations placed upon their freedom of action and the genuine threats to the safety of themselves and their children if they took any action. Furthermore, their decisions can only be understood if the high value they placed on the relationships and the high expectations they had for the fulfillment of their own emotional needs and for the provision of security for their children are properly acknowledged.

Most of the women in the survey group had left the relationship more than once before our interviews. Only four of the women we interviewed had never left their partners. It was the first time of leaving for 11 others. Most, though, had left their homes from two to six times before, and three women said they had left home about ten times previously. Many of these women faced great difficulties in getting support because they had left before and then took their partners back to try again. When the violence restarted and they left again, the women found they were not taken seriously by agencies. One such woman went back to the Housing Executive the second time she left her husband. *"They said I had been separated from him before and I went back to him, so they said I must have been telling lies. So I had a terrible time proving that I didn't make myself intentionally homeless."* For others, the fear that they wouldn't get help the second or third time around made women stay longer in the violent relationship.

Much emphasis in the literature and in professional practice is placed on an examination of the reasons why some women do not act to stop the violence and leave the relationship. One social worker in our study suggested that that is the wrong question. She thought equal emphasis should be placed on the other side of the equation by asking why men keep coming back. Men's insistence on coming back to their partners was a major problem for many of the women in our study. Thirty-five per cent (20) had experienced violence after they had left their partners. Several others lived with the constant fear that partners would attack them if they were found. Some of these women had to leave their homes in England and the Republic and return to their original communities in Northern Ireland. Often they would have had more support remaining near their marital home, rather than coming back to Northern Ireland. But, as one woman explained, *"I knew from the last time he was in the same area as me, and I still never got no peace. I just can't be in the same country as him. I just have to stay out of the way completely."* Others had to leave Northern Ireland to escape their former partners. Yet other women, while remaining in Northern Ireland, had to break all connections with communities and families and 'disappear' or go 'underground.'

This option presented enormous difficulties for all women who had previously had a family and social network for support. But it was particularly problematic for women from the Travellers and Asian communities. The feelings of separation from their distinct cultural groups and the loss of friends and social networks were exacerbated by the experience of moving into an alien, settled or English speaking, environment. The isolating effects of such experiences has influenced many such women to return to their abusive partners.

Women explained that they had not acted sooner because of feelings of shame and pride, fear of their partners and because of concern for their children. The largest group of responses (18) to this question centred around women's own attitudes (see table 7, Annex 2). Feelings of shame, pride and self-blame deterred them from making the issue public by leaving. Women also pointed to their own lack of confidence and their fear that no-one would believe them if they did tell about the violence.

Sixteen responses related to women's fears for their children – both fears for their security and fears that they would lose the children if they exposed the violence. *"I kept thinking the kids need stability."* Several women expressed fears about raising the children in a lone parent family, as one said, "*I always felt it wasn't fair for the children to have no father.*"

Fear of their partners' reactions if they left or got help was cited in 13 responses. Women explained that they were afraid the violence would get worse or that partners would carry out their threats to kill women if they left. This reason given by women is often not understood by professionals who want to help abused women. That is, the reason why it is expected that a woman should leave the violence is simultaneously the reason why she does not. As shown in the examples of continuing violence discussed above, women's fears are reasonable and a logical consequence of this is that it may take a longer time for women to reach a decision.

Expectations regarding the future, belief in their partner's promises to change, and confidence that the women could handle it themselves was another set of explanations given. Objective factors such as lack of information, money and housing, and fear of their families' reaction stopped other women from acting. Several young women who had married or cohabited against their family's wishes stayed in particularly violent relationships because they did not want to have their families saying 'I told you so' when the marriage failed.

Women's emotional attachment to the partner and their conditioning and acceptance of violence as the norm for their lives were the responses given by only a small minority of women. One woman gave this reason for staying as long as she did. "*I loved him with all my heart. I used to wish I didn't love him but I did.*"

When it came finally to taking action, the main impetus was not usually a particular episode of violence. For most it was realising that things were not going to change and deciding that they had had enough. For 19 women, it was the recognition that 'I can't take any more', 'my nerves are wrecked.'

Their children featured in the decision of 12 women finally to take action. They left because their partners started hitting the children, because the children were emotionally affected and because of the bad example of violent behaviour that was being set for them.

The actual violence, the dangers posed to pregnant women and the fear of future violence were the reasons given by 11 women. Other women gave reasons apart from the violence: seven cited their husbands' affairs and three cited the need for money. One of the women who filed for separation orders for the sole purpose of getting court maintenance orders explained, *"I actually went and got a separation for to get money. I had to get money from somewhere."* One woman left when she finally convinced her family about the violence and another waited until her mother died before she felt able to leave.

Family Responses

As indicated above, families were usually the first and most consistent source of support for women who had experienced domestic violence. Generally, the families of the women in this survey were very supportive of their daughters when they were eventually told about the violence. However, women's own reluctance to tell and family attitudes and concerns could serve as a deterrent. Some never told their families and others only told their families after putting up with the violence for a long period of time. Concern for families was the main reason for this reluctance. Women did not want to worry or hurt the families; they knew they had other problems like illnesses in the family; and they did not want to place the families in physical danger from their violent husbands.

After overcoming the reluctance to tell, several women found that at first families did not believe them and had to be convinced about the violence. One father reacted to his daughter's reports of the violence by threatening her himself. It was not until he actually saw her injuries and had to care for her himself that he believed what she had been saying. One mother would not believe her son-in-law was not the "perfect man" she had imagined. Several women told of the shame their families felt about marriages splitting up. One of those is not welcome in her mother's house because of the 'disgrace' she has brought to the family. *"They don't like telling neighbours or people that their daughter's marriage is broken up. I am not allowed to go down to my mum's house . . . she doesn't want the neighbours to see me without a husband."*

Both Catholic and Protestant women had problems because of the religious beliefs of their families. One Catholic father was more upset when the violent husband reported that his wife was using birth control than he was about the way her husband was abusing her. Another woman still suffers from her Protestant father's condemnation of her because he is opposed to divorce. Four years after her marriage ended, he still thinks she should return to the marital home in spite of the violence.

When women did finally tell their families, the most frequent help provided was accommodation, taking the woman into the family home. Several helped their daughters make contact with a refuge, others suggested they contact a social worker. Several families either retaliated physically against the partner or wanted to do so; others went to talk to the partner. Such actions often led to family members being beaten up by the husband, deterring women from going back to their families for further support.

In terms of advice given to women, families overwhelmingly suggested that women 'get out' or 'leave him.' There were a few who told women to 'go back, make it work.' Other families said they would support any decision their daughter made, an attitude which these women found to be very helpful. Several women told of the frustration their families felt when they went back to their violent partners. Others reported that parents said they wanted to do something earlier, but felt their daughter would not let them.

While the women's families provided support, the same cannot be said about their partners' families. Only one man's family was reported as supportive. Several women told of criticisms and attacks heaped upon them when they left their partners. Parents, particularly mothers, tended to minimise the harm caused by their sons. Some mothers-in-law had looked to wives to care for their sons and to keep them out of trouble, showing little concern for their daughters-in-law's fate. *"Whenever I got him arrested, his mother said, 'Sure he only hit you with an ashtray.' I got stitches. She wants me to protect him but I need protected from him."* When another woman ended up in hospital because of the injuries, her in-laws said *"if he did hit her, he couldn't hit her that hard."* Not surprisingly, the women were upset by these attitudes which may reflect the general lack of concern about domestic violence and the lack of community condemnation of men who assault women in the home.

Northern Ireland Factors

Is domestic violence differently perceived or differently received in Northern Ireland? We consider here both religious factors and social attitudes more generally.

Clergy

Because of the high level of religious participation in Northern Ireland and the important role played by the churches in matters concerning morals and the family, it was expected that the clergy might be an important contact for women seeking guidance and support. Women were asked about responses from clergy in order to examine the extent to which traditional church attitudes in Northern Ireland impinged on women's decision-making process. Forty-one per cent (23) of the women in the sample said they were in contact with clergy. Women from the Catholic community had a higher level of contact, with 44 per cent (15) responding on this question compared to 36 per cent (eight) of the women from the Protestant community. Only seven of the contacts reported by the women were seen as helpful. Protestant women expressed less satisfaction, with only two positive responses compared to five Catholic women who described a helpful response from clergy. Some women explained that they knew what to expect, so they didn't go to the clergy. *"I know my priest would probably try to talk you round... you have to stay in there no matter what. I don't want them to tell me that because I've done that for too long."*

In practice, when women went to clergy for advice or support, an equal number of women were given advice to leave the relationship as were told to stay and make a go of it. A few Catholics were assisted by supportive priests, but most had particular difficulty because of the Catholic church's opposition to divorce and remarriage. Several of the priests, while they supported the woman in leaving her partner, would insist that 'you'll still be married'. However increased pain and distress was often the result of such contacts. Only a few women we spoke to stayed in violent marriages because of clerical attitudes, but in these cases the process of leaving was more stressful and the period of healing after the break-up was particularly painful and extensive.

As other research has shown (McLaughlin 1991), when their position in the family is challenged, men look to, and receive from the church, affirmation of the moral authority they expect as husband/father in the family. In this study, men did go to the clergy, and enlisted the minister or priest to convince the women to take them back. When a priest came out at the behest of one husband, he just talked to the woman's father who then convinced her to take her husband back. Although the priest and the father knew about the violence, the priest did not bother to talk directly to the woman. In the several examples of mixed marriages we had in our sample, husbands did not go to the cleric of their own religion, but to their wife's priest or minister in order to put pressure on her. One Catholic man sent a minister to visit his partner in a refuge. The minister, she reported, had said that *"God is making all the things happen to me, to stop living in sin. God is punishing me."*

Refusal to believe women and defence of men was a common response by clergy. Sometimes other transgressions committed by the husband, such as adultery, made more of an impression on priests. Some ministers tried to explain the husband's behaviour, 'he's insecure', 'he has a drink problem', or made promises on behalf of the man, 'he won't do it again.' Others either refused to help or did not want to get involved. Some just offered to pray for the couple or blessed them. Disappointments were particularly severe for those women who turned to religion for support after they had ended their relationships. One Presbyterian woman became a communicant after she left her husband and lost custody of her children. She felt the need of spiritual support during this crisis in her life, but her minister was not ready to assist her by discussing the problem.

Attitudes

Women's stories about making decisions to get help or to leave home also illustrate the barriers imposed by social and religious attitudes in Northern Ireland. The survey of social attitudes in Northern Ireland found support for the view that Northern Ireland is a more traditional society than Britain. The survey showed that attitudes in Northern Ireland are conservative on issues such as pre-marital sexual relationships, abortion and divorce and that women were more opposed than men to further liberalisation of divorce in Northern Ireland (Montgomery and Davies 1991). This may reflect Northern Ireland women's lower participation in the labour market than in Great Britain and the centrality of marriage and family in women's lives.

The interviews in this study supported these findings, even among the younger women in the group. The most common religious belief that affected women's decisions was the idea that marriage is for-ever. "You make your bed, you lie in it," was a view repeated over and over again. Specific objections to divorce were mentioned by several women, *"I suppose being brought up a Catholic, I felt when I got married, that was it. You know, it was an awful thing to break up your marriage, and maybe subconsciously, that was probably maybe why I did hang in for so long."* Others separated and went back because of their opposition to divorce. *"This is going to lead to divorce, I can't do this. So I went back and took more abuse, just because I didn't want a divorce. I'm still pretty anti-divorce, but I can't see any other way out anymore."*

Religion was not always the basis of the objection to divorce. As one explained, *"Well I believe that marriage is for life and you worked at it. Religion wasn't a lot to do with it. I never believed in divorce. I thought it was an easy option. I thought it was just other people's way of moving from one relationship to another. I never seen myself getting a divorce. Maybe being widowed..."* For many women, then, religious or not, marriage was serious and you had to work at it.

The attachment to marriage and the family was even more strongly emphasised by the Traveller women. They said a woman's life centred around her children, *"All we believe in is our home and children."* One woman explained, *"Travelling women have a very strict life with the one husband. When we get married, that's for life. It's not easy to separate".* The women also explained that even if they did separate they would never take another partner. *"Say you were away for years and years. We'd never take up with another man. The men might take with other women, but the women would never take up with another man. It's not because it's Catholic, it's the Travellers way. A very strict way."*

Because they wanted to make their marriages work, the women would try again and again and hope for change. And when it did not work, the women felt they were failures. *"Leaving would be admitting defeat, maybe I could have tried harder."* This attitude was often encouraged by husbands. As one woman said, *"He had me convinced at that time, that it was my fault. That I was no good as a wife, as a mother, I was a slut, a whore."*

Public admission of the failure of the marriage, which the women considered to be their fault, was particularly difficult. Women felt that their mistakes and guilt was exposed to public view. *"I felt as if I was standing naked in the middle of Belfast. That I was completely stripped to the bone, after having a happy family, sort of people thinking that, I was completely naked, and everybody could see into my very soul, because it had all fallen down around me."* Even though they were the victims, the women felt they would be blamed for the breakup and they felt no one would believe their stories. *"Nobody would believe, if they met him, that he was a violent person. He was so good hearted, so kind, so happy go lucky. He was the life and the soul of the party."* Many women showed photos of their good looking husbands and boy-friends and described their good points. The fact that they appeared to be ordinary decent men made it much more difficult to convince others that when they came home, they were violent. Women thought, and expected others to think, that in some way they were themselves to blame.

The women also said that there were stigmas against lone parent families, separated and divorced women, women who had been victims of domestic violence, and women who had lost custody of their children. Both single mothers and separated women expressed the view that there was a stigma against lone parent families. *"You do feel different in society. People do look down on one parent families to a certain extent…most people don't understand."*

Other women thought that public attitudes to domestic violence was the basis of a community stigma. Because domestic violence is still viewed as an individual problem, some women did not feel that it was a universal problem. *"I thought it was something to do with me and him. I didn't realise it was so widespread."* This woman felt this contributed to people looking down on her. The impact of this stigma on the victims of the violence was reflected in the number of women who referred to feelings of shame, embarrassment and awkwardness that made them reluctant to get help or leave the relationship.

Losing custody of children after leaving violent husbands brought a double burden – the loss of their children and the condemnation of society. *"Perhaps it's that I imagine people are thinking what sort of woman is that who didn't get custody of her children? I was punished and I continue to be punished and it is making me feel guilty."*

Attitudes reflecting the notion of a privatised family and a rejection of outside interference were very common in the interviews. This was common to middle class women: *"my background would have been discretion, you never spoke to anybody about it,"* and working class women: *"you don't go to outsiders."* This attitude was a definite limitation on women's ability to go to professional agencies for support. One woman was under pressure from her own family and from her in-laws. *"I just could never go and make that first step to go and get help. His mother, she's the type of woman that any problems you have, you keep them inside the home, you just don't go outside the family."* In her case, when her husband beat her up in public, it wasn't the violence her mother-in-law was concerned about, but the public nature of it. They were told, *"The two of youse are always letting yourselves down. You should have kept it from outside."*

There is an acceptance of domestic violence in local communities which limits both the opportunities to intervene and women's ability to go to outside agencies. The ambivalent attitude toward the beating of women, was experienced by one woman when she was being beaten outside a pub, and she heard one of the men saying, *"It's a man and wife, leave it."* Fortunately for her, another man disagreed and intervened to help her. Several other women thought their neighbours must have known what was happening but never did anything to help either while the violence was occurring or afterwards.

One woman, however, found tremendous support in her working class area once she made the violence public and left her partner. A very well organised community network of support acknowledged the fine line that is drawn between public support and the private nature of the family. One community worker explained that neighbours will not interfere unless it is clear that the woman wants to do something. *"The position is that if a woman's husband came back to harass her now, I would say, en masse, the neighbours would be out. Because she's made the move and she's made the decision that she doesn't want him there. But while she has him there, they won't interfere."* One woman got tremendous support when, after she had escaped from her partner, he abducted one of their children. *"It was an invisible network, a network I didn't know was there."* In such a situation the community, by respecting the private nature of the family, is placing all the onus on the woman to take the first step. But this is the most difficult step to take and women are often not aware of the support that can be there for them.

Impact of the Troubles

Women were asked if the political situation or the 'Troubles' in Northern Ireland had affected their decisions or ability to get help. They were also specifically asked if the political situation affected their attitude to contacting the police and if paramilitaries had become involved in any way.

The biggest problem reported by the women was their perceived inability to make contact with the police about the domestic violence. Women said *"the police won't answer calls, the RUC thinks they are being set up."* This perception affected women living in nationalist sections in both urban and rural areas.

There was little indication that there would be community disapproval in nationalist areas if women did contact the police, although one woman reported she was warned by others not to bring the police in. Another was upset about what the neighbours would say when the police helicopter landed in a field in answer to her call. There was, however, a greater sense that the police are *"not there to help you."* When we asked women if they would contact the armed patrols as they came down the street, the response was *"they are not there to help. In this area police are not people that you normally go to. I mean, to walk out and stop them on the street, they would laugh at you – I mean they don't have any contact with this community whatsoever"*. Another woman explained that they do not go to the police because *"we look after ourselves. When we look for help, the police are never included. They are always seen as to be the harasser"*. In another community, women expressed the fear that if they reported men to the police because of domestic violence, the police might try to recruit them as informers.

So if some women are reluctant or unable to contact the police, do they go to alternative and available sources of help from paramilitary organisations to force partners to stop the violence? Only four women in the survey said that paramilitary groups got involved and there was only one case in which action was taken. Several women knew they could go to them for help but one woman thought the IRA in her area would take the attitude, *"We don't like getting involved."*

The initiative to consult paramilitaries came primarily from families, neighbours and from paramilitary groups themselves. But one woman who did go to the UDA (Ulster Defence Association) herself found they got her partner out of the house, *"quicker than the police."* But she is now afraid that the UDA might expect something in return. In most cases the women who considered involving paramilitaries, decided against it, mostly because they did not want their partners to be physically harmed. One husband had already been threatened by the IRA for petty crime and his wife *"knew they are looking for an excuse to do him, but I wouldn't have that on my conscience. But if I thought they could advise him – I would have gone to them and said he won't leave me alone. But they go too far."* When another women got no support from the police, the UDA offered to do something about her husband. *"They would have give him the same as he gives me."* She refused their help *"so that he can't claim I did him any harm."*

The availability of guns, both legal and illegal, was another problem raised in interviews. Women thought there was reluctance on the part of police to remove legally held weapons from men who were abusing and threatening their partners.

The women also pointed to problems in getting rehoused and the lack of mixed housing estates as a factor related to the 'Troubles'. Certainly women who want to be rehoused back into Catholic West Belfast face long waiting lists and may have to settle for areas away from their families because of the pressure on housing in that area. But women in other areas discussed the problem in getting an estate of the 'right religion'. They had to spend longer time in refuges and some found their emergency status threatened if they refused houses in the 'wrong estates.' One woman indicated the need for more integrated schools and mixed housing estates.

Special Needs

Rural women are one group whose needs are distinctive. While most of the women in our survey lived in urban areas, nine women did come from rural areas or small towns. They indicated particular problems that need to be highlighted. As with other women, there was intense pressure to keep the problems in the family, but it was more difficult to do that in a rural area because of the close family and community ties. Because of the scarcity of support networks outside the extended family, the family circle loomed larger, both as temporary support for women, but also as pressure on the women to maintain their marriage. Women thought it would be easier to deal with domestic violence in a town because *"here they keep their private sides more than if you live in a town or city."*

Leaving a marriage was a more difficult option for rural women because *"everyone knows"*. One woman who left her husband because of his adultery felt shameful because *"I live in a small town and people know our families. The hardest thing is going into the shops and wondering what's being said."* A combination of class attitudes and the lack of privacy had an important impact on another woman's decision because she and her husband ran businesses in a small town. She thought that people only expected violence in marriages on housing estates and looked down on her because it happened to her.

In the smaller towns and rural areas, there are fewer community support groups between the family and the statutory agencies, leaving women with less access to information and support. But we found that women were reluctant to use whatever support agencies are available. One woman explained, *"I think in a rural area, you are not inclined to contact some place, where you feel it is going to be your next door neighbour that you are talking to whenever you ring up."* Volunteers working with the Catholic Marriage Advisory Council took this attitude into account by assigning their advisors to areas other than their own towns. It is important that women be made aware of this practice. Currently, the lack of available support and the fear that their neighbours will be involved, means that many women do travel to Belfast for advice.

As well as community attitudes in rural areas, lack of local resources, limited access to transport, and inadequate housing provision increase the impediments for women. Women tend to live further away from available refuges and there are fewer Housing Executive hostels. Those women who know that the local hotel is the only available housing option for them are quite likely to endure the violence for a longer period. In order to go to a refuge, they may have to change the children's schools and to leave their own areas, cutting themselves off from social networks that may be important, particularly when they try to begin independent lives.

Special problems facing minority women were also raised in the interviews. These suggest the need to recognise that there are more than two traditions in Northern Ireland. Provision of services based on the assumption that clients are settled and English-speaking ignores the needs of women from other cultures. The gap in service provision for two ethnic groups was apparent in the research and their needs are considered here. These are the Travelling community which has endured a long history of discrimination and public neglect and the Asian community, a newer group in Northern Ireland.

Traveller women were interviewed in refuges and in their homes on sites. Their experiences are incorporated throughout the body of this report, but the issue of domestic violence and the Travellers merits consideration in its own right. Popular attitudes have labelled the Travellers as being particularly prone to violence but there is no evidence to suggest that domestic violence is any more common in the Travelling community than in the settled community. However, racist attitudes towards them and their desire to maintain their particular way of life in the light of government policy which offers options only in the settled community, has meant that Traveller women have fewer options when domestic violence does occur. They have found difficulty in respite provision, resettlement, and the lack of support from professionals.

Traveller women did praise the development of Women's Aid and made comparisons with the past when women would huddle with all their children under a caravan or in a ditch to get away from violent husbands. Many Traveller women now use both the Housing Executive accommodation and Women's Aid as a temporary respite against the violence in their homes, but the pressures they encounter force many of them to return to violent partners at an early stage. Racist attitudes from other women, forced separation from their children because of lack of accommodation, accusations of theft, and fear that their children would not be accepted were but some of the difficulties highlighted.

A particular feature of the Traveller women's experience was the constant harassment from their husbands which they endured while they were in refuges. Traveller husbands have an extensive network of support to find and threaten their wives. Their presence for long hours outside a refuge is a source of fear for these women who become virtual prisoners inside the house. This pressure forces many to go to refuges far from their own communities. Also to avoid these problems, Women's Aid tries to take only one Traveller family per refuge. While this practice may provide better protection for all the women in the refuge, it results in greater isolation for the one woman Traveller. Most women also do not want to be rehoused in the settled community, but even those who do accept this option find the long waiting list and the difficulty involved in being designated homeless an additional problem.

A special refuge as an additional option for Traveller women has been suggested to overcome some of the problems. Northern Ireland Women's Aid Federation and the Northern Ireland Council for

Travelling People have indicated that such a "Traveller-only refuge" would be particularly suitable for those Traveller women who have been going in and out of refuges over a period of time. These women have made a definite choice to leave their partners, but have found it difficult to adjust to life outside the Travelling community. Long term, safe, second stage housing would help these Traveller women avoid returning to violent homes.

Representatives of the Chinese Welfare Association discussed the particular difficulties facing Asian women who suffer domestic violence in Northern Ireland. This is a large and growing community, including 7,000 to 8,000 Chinese people, mostly living in the greater Belfast area. Fears about immigration status, lack of knowledge of benefit rights and language difficulties are important deterrents for women attempting to leave violent husbands. Because a large percentage of the women do not speak English, the need for Chinese language leaflets and available interpreters for help providers is acute, particularly when the issue is one of domestic violence. The difficulties faced by women have raised serious concerns for their safety.

In addition to the language difficulties, their work which is often in a family business with their husbands and the lack of an extended family in Northern Ireland, leave the women particularly dependent on their husbands with few alternatives to staying in violent marriages. Their many problems are acknowledged in Britain where there are Asian women's refuges, Chinese women's helplines and leaflets in Chinese and other languages and it is important that similar measures be introduced in Northern Ireland.

Starting Again, Support and Advice

Loneliness and support for their children were the problems women had or expected to have once they began living on their own. Several women already had the experience of leaving partners and talked about the loneliness which had pressurised some women into taking violent partners back. A few women said they would like to stay in touch with a social worker or health visitor, *"so I don't feel really depressed and down, which I know I'm going to be, on my own."*

Women talked about the difficulties they expected when they left the refuge with all its support. *"When you are here you get into the hostel's way – it's a big step to get out of that routine. Every night there is something for the kids to do – disco, swimming, baking. My kids will go up the walls when they move out of here. Plus there is always company – always someone to talk to. When you move into a new house, you are back on your own again and it will be lonely."* Women's Aid refuges hold meetings in the evenings or during the day for ex-residents to participate in, but many women are rehoused too far away to take advantage of it.

Many of the women had lost their confidence through the years of violence and found it difficult to make new friends and to join new groups. Some local women's and Gingerbread groups are trying to overcome women's reluctance to come to new groups on their own by taking a more active role in approaching new women, particularly lone parents, in the area. Women's other important concern was the effects of both the violence and the upheaval on their children. As one said, *"There is children in school going through sheer hell"*. Several women had tried to get help for problems their children had, but they were not successful.

There were several references to problems regarding access arrangements and the continued threat to women's safety after relationships had ended. Hester and Radford (1992) have discussed the need to consider the safety of women and children involved in divorce and separation. This is essential in view of the increasing emphasis on conciliation and mediation and the focus on shared responsibility between parents in the Children Act 1989, which does not mention the problem of domestic violence. Since several of the women in this study indicated they had problems under current arrangements, it is essential that this question be addressed in the consultation process for the Children Order (Northern Ireland, Draft Order 1993).

Concerns for their future economic security and difficulties in obtaining community care grants for resettlement were also discussed. Increased pressure was expected with the implementation of the new Child Support Act particularly in view of reports of attacks on women who have named putative fathers.

In their interviews with us, women gave advice for others in the same situation and made several suggestions for improving the support for abused women. These were:

- Women should "get out" or "get rid of him". This was the most frequent advice given. Women should go to the police, social workers or phone Women's Aid and they assured women that *"you don't have to take it"*.

- More publicity was necessary to raise general awareness about domestic violence. *"Don't keep it hidden, bring it out in the open"*, was what women said. Special programmes for teenagers in schools were suggested in order to teach about the realities of marriage and to show that men and boys have "no right to be violent".

- There should be more training for professionals and special social workers for domestic violence.

- There were proposals for tougher sentences, changes in the courts, and assertiveness classes for women.

- Full support at weekends, a phone line at night, more women's centres, and counselling programmes for women who lose custody were other suggestions.

These interviews have revealed at close quarters just what domestic violence means to women who are on the receiving end of it. It is repeated, serious, physical abuse that can threaten their health and can put their very lives at risk. It is damage to their psychological well-being, to their sense of self-worth and ability to take control of their lives. It can have serious, sometimes long term effects on children. It can sometimes extend, if they interfere, to members of the woman's wider family. The route out of a violent situation is neither easy nor straightforward. Debates about explanations can degenerate into victim-blaming. There can be community censure as well as community support. Health and social services professionals are not often the first resort but their role can be a crucial one. We have just seen that the women themselves call for more training and for a specialist group of social workers. In the next chapter, we consider the more specific comments the women make on different groups of help-providers and compare these with our interviews with the providers themselves.

FOUR

Statutory Sector: Experiences and Responses

We have already seen from the women's accounts that there is a large number of agencies and professionals dealing with domestic violence and no clear allocation of responsibility to any one of them. Health and social service staff based in the four health centres in the urban and rural sample areas as well as professionals in hospitals, family centres and other units in these areas were interviewed. Many of the interviews with abused women took place in these areas (Annex 1), but the match is not an exact one, therefore no inference can be drawn that any of the women's comments refer to specific professionals in any locality. We asked the professionals about the extent of domestic violence in their practice and about their responses to women who were experiencing abuse. The interviews also dealt with problems encountered and referrals made to other agencies. We included questions about guidelines on domestic violence and on the amount of training received. Suggestions for the way forward in this area of work were also recorded.

Women had a high level of contact with the services and groups covered in this chapter. Nearly two-thirds had seen social workers, the Housing Executive, and the police, and over 50 per cent went to see their GPs. Health visitors saw 45 per cent of the women in the sample and 39 per cent went to Accident and Emergency. There was a much lower level of contact with the other professional agencies. These response rates are comparable to rates found in British studies and higher than those found in Evason's Northern Ireland study (1982) and Ruddle and O'Connor's (1992) study in the Republic.

The chapter is in two main sections. Section One deals with professionals within the main health and social service agencies, covering social workers, doctors, accident and emergency staffs and health visitors and also including those who deal with specific features of domestic violence in Mental Health Units and Alcohol Abuse Units. Section Two deals with other statutory agencies, the police, the judicial system, the Probation Service and the Housing Executive.

For each group, we summarise the extent to which women used the agency and their overall view of the helpfulness of it, moving on to examine the responses of help-providers. Given that the decision agreed with the funders was to provide a broad brush picture and to cover as many services as possible, we do not claim to provide an in-depth study of any one professional group and the comments we report here, do not necessarily reflect the profession as a whole. Nonetheless, the picture which emerges gives coherence to the women's views and also points to the way forward on domestic violence.

SECTION ONE: HEALTH AND SOCIAL SERVICES

Social Workers

Social workers have a statutory responsibility for protecting children, but no similar responsibility for the care and protection of women, except in cases of mental illness, disability, and elderly care. The Home Office Report on domestic violence (Smith 1989) pointed out that social workers, because of their training, ought to be able to help abused women. Smith found, however, a marked reluctance among social workers to take an active role. Our interviews with women showed a perception of social workers without an active concern about women. Since they have the power to take children into care, the controlling, rather than the caring, aspect of social work often had a greater impact on women.

Women's Experiences

Although a majority of the women were eventually in contact with social workers, there was a marked reluctance to approach them. Some of this was due to fear of partners but, in both group and individual interviews, women emphasised their fear of having children removed if social workers knew about the violence.

Ignoring the violence against the women and showing concern only for the children was the main reason given by women who said the social worker was not helpful. *"She made me feel that I wasn't looking after the kids when we were arguing, but she never asked how badly I was hurt"*. Others thought the advice was not helpful when they were told *"to get rid of him"* or *"to get back together and talk"*. Some women said they were told there was nothing they could do about the situation whilst others found it difficult to talk to the social workers because they seemed too young and inexperienced and others found a problem with the social workers' attitudes. There was dissatisfaction with social work responses that centred around the children. Several women reported that the social worker threatened to remove their children if they remained with their partner. In spite of the statutory responsibility social workers have for children, there were many examples given in which children's needs and safety were overlooked in cases of domestic violence. For instance, when one woman went to a refuge, she was worried about leaving her oldest daughter behind because her husband had on occasions also been physically abusive towards the girl. Rather than supporting the woman's concern, the social worker thought it was appropriate for the daughter to remain in the home with her father.

Less than one-third of the women found contact with social workers to be helpful. However, their experiences illustrate the vital role that can be played by this service in assisting women to escape from the violence. For example, after years with a social worker who never offered advice about the violence, one woman was able to make a real change after a new worker was assigned to her case. Her new social worker asked about the violence because "*I had scars over my body from him hitting me,*" and told her about refuges. "*I think if I knew about Women's Aid years and years ago, I maybe woulda been out of it*".

Suggestions made by women included the provision of specialist social workers for domestic violence cases, that women should not be passed around from one social worker to the next and that women should be consulted on the social workers assigned to them.

Social Worker Experiences

We interviewed 16 social workers in the sample areas. The majority were in Family and Child Care work, and the remainder dealt with mental illness, alcoholism, and elderly care. There was a marked divergence in social work attitudes toward the definition, causes and responsibility for domestic violence. Those who emphasised individual or pathological explanations for domestic violence were less likely to be on the alert for domestic violence and were more satisfied with current social service provisions. A minority rejected pathological explanations, were more likely to presume a higher prevalence of domestic violence, were more critical of current social service provisions and much more likely to suggest that social services should focus on the needs of women. In some areas it appeared that there was a relationship between social work attitudes, the level of social deprivation, and the perception of the prevalence of domestic violence in the case load.

There were no social work policies or guidelines specifically relating to domestic violence. One manager argued that there was an informal policy, but nothing on paper, while others queried how guidelines on domestic violence would relate to their specific areas of work.

None of the units had social workers who were recognised as having particular expertise on domestic violence, though some individuals had a personal interest in the issue. The social workers had little or no pre-vocational or in-service training on domestic violence. The inadequacy of social work training in this area prompted one social worker to say, *"The reality of working with domestic violence victims is different from anything you would get on a social work course."* Most were very definite on the need for training. One social worker argued for particular training for women social workers both for their work with clients and for their own emotional needs as workers dealing with these problems. In addition to this, others argued for longer social work training periods.

Social workers in the Family and Child care teams came across domestic violence primarily through cases already on the books, with some referrals from police, neighbours and teachers. These teams usually only become involved in domestic violence when children were affected or involved. For social workers in the mental health field, the presenting issue could be a range of problems such as depression, anxiety, eating disorders, or child management. Domestic violence was also regularly found in alcohol abuse work and in elderly care. Concerns for the elderly were raised by a number of community workers, social workers, and members of women's groups. Much of the concern related to abusing carers, often the children of the elderly person. However social workers have found that violence by an elderly spouse does occur as well. They have found cases where there is a pattern of violence, with the violence recurring for 40 or 50 years, and endured by the woman. However, as one social worker indicated, elderly women are less able to sustain the injuries the older they get.

The incidence of domestic violence was not monitored by any of the social work units in this study; therefore estimates of the occurrence of domestic violence in the case load differed widely, even within one office. All statements could well be underestimates (cf Maynard 1985). The differing perception may be due to social work focus, particularly in family and child care, on responsibility for children, rather than adults. Domestic violence is also getting lost in the present organisational structure of social work. As there is no area in social work responsible for domestic violence, if a woman phoned up and said *"my husband is beating me, I don't have any children, I am under sixty five, I am not physically disabled and I'm not mentally ill"*, the case would not be picked up as a referral. Such a woman would probably be re-directed to Women's Aid by the duty social worker.

Finding the domestic violence during an assessment is dependent on the skills and attitudes of the individual social worker. We found a definite reluctance amongst many of the social workers interviewed to assume that domestic violence might be a problem for a client or to address the issue at an early interview. Despite the fact that most of the social workers thought their role included being on the alert for domestic violence, a number of social workers said they would not ask directly about domestic violence when they were taking a family history in a case of child abuse. Even when domestic violence was suspected, some of the social workers said they might not, or not necessarily, ask directly about domestic violence. But other social workers said they would just *"presume"* domestic violence was occurring and ask directly. One of these thought *"we should be asking about domestic violence. We could improve and have a more holistic approach."* She thought that men who are sex abusers abuse in other ways, but in the social work assessment the question of physical abuse is focussed on the child.

Where women disclosed domestic violence, the initial responses of the social workers to women were to let them talk or 'ventilate', and then go through the options that were available. One social worker said she would counsel the woman and show how her behaviour provoked the violence. Generally information and advice given included police contacts, solicitors and exclusion and protection orders, and Women's Aid. Most social workers stressed that women had to make their own decisions and were not prepared to be more proactive despite women wanting direction. But a few social workers said they would take a proactive stance, discuss the negative aspects if the woman stays in the situation, and say, *"you don't have to put up with it"*.

All of the social workers recognised women's fear of their statutory powers to have children taken into care. However, they stressed that it was essential to assess the impact on the children even if the children were not being directly abused. Most of the social workers were very aware of, and had experience with, children who had suffered because of violence in their homes. It was also posed as a problem for the future, *"because children who see their mothers being physically abused, sometimes they perpetuate that behaviour, and become violent to their mothers and sisters"*. Given the level of concern and the statutory responsibility for childcare, it was somewhat contradictory that there were few available specialist services such as counselling for children who are living in violent homes.

In spite of the awareness of the effect of domestic violence on children, family and child care social workers expressed difficulty with the idea of doing more to highlight domestic violence. They tended to view this suggestion as 'adding domestic violence on' to the work of family and child care, rather than agreeing to the integral nature of the issue for this work. Most thought domestic violence should not be taken on by family and child care teams, while some suggested that there needed to be a specialist service for domestic violence outside of this area because they wanted to retain the focus on children. It was also argued that social workers were not ignoring domestic violence, they were just overwhelmed by it and that social services couldn't cope with the numbers if they were responsible for domestic violence cases. Another thought social workers were frustrated about their inability to help because of the lack of support from other agencies, such as the police or housing. But the most common difficulty discussed was frustration because women stay in the situation or go back to violent partners. Several social workers felt helpless when in spite of all the information, advice and support, women *"still allowed it to happen to them, again and again and again"*.

- *Funding for training, including interdisciplinary training, on all issues related to domestic violence.*

- *Assigning only more mature, experienced and well trained social workers to domestic violence cases.*

- *Greater involvement of social services with the community or voluntary sector in developing specialist teams to deal with domestic violence.* Some thought a community oriented team would be most useful to provide a service geared to the needs of women.

- *The development of public awareness* through publicity and general community education about violence against elderly women.

- *Resources for more regular counselling,* including attachment to a family on a longer term basis.

Social workers also provided a number of comments suggesting examples of good practice which could well be used in training and for developing guidelines. Some of these have been collected together and are outlined below.

Social Workers' Examples of Good Practice

1. Non judgmental practice

"I listen to what she wants first of all. I point out she can get an exclusion order. I ask generally how she is. A lot of women know they should be leaving the situation but they can't at that particular moment of time. And I acknowledge that's all right. I don't pressurise any woman. I may feel that she should do that, but I don't do that, because that'd put more pressure on the woman. I just listen to what she has to say. I point out the consequences for herself of staying, or of leaving, in as nice a way as I can."

2. Take women to visit a hostel

"Sometimes I've taken women over to a hostel, and say, OK this is happening on a regular basis, now we'll take you over to the hostel, we'll make an appointment for you to come to meet the people in the hostel, and then whenever it occurs again, maybe this is an option."

3. Avoid labelling

Every client is an individual and shouldn't be labelled. Just because a woman is going back again to the same situation doesn't mean that she must like it.

4. Confront the violent partner

"I went down and said that it was totally unacceptable what he did. He was very violent. She wanted to go into the house so I said he must give us a guarantee that he won't come back."

5. Place a family aid

"They're like a home help, but they're there all the time. The abused woman had five children and she signed herself out of hospital. So we had to have somebody there to make sure the children had meals and that she had some protection against him."

6. Treat people with respect

"No matter if they abuse their children sexually, there's a certain common decency and courtesy in the way you speak to people. We do not abuse our power."

7. Urgency required

All situations of violence require an urgent response.

8. Feeling safe

Provide the opportunity for the woman "to build the relationship so that she will feel safe enough to disclose the violence and know that you are not going to make a value judgment."

9. Using male models

"One particular fella, in one of the cases he was brilliant, because he was able to provide a role model . . . this is how men act. You don't have to accept it."

10. Provide after care

"We would contact the local women's group or some of the community groups, just to make sure that there is a social network for them to tie into. There is also an open door policy, whereas at any stage they feel, 'I really need to tap into that resource again', they can come back to us."

General Practitioners

One might assume that the local health centre or doctor's surgery would become a focal point for women in the help seeking process since those with young children often have to attend for vaccinations and regular check-ups. The literature also shows that women visit GPs for a variety of medical complaints frequently related to domestic violence. The availability then of the local doctor and the specific medical problems associated with the abuse makes the GP an important part of the help-seeking process.

Reluctance to tell about the violence governed women's involvement with medical care. Feelings of fear and shame were the main reasons given by women (15) when asked why they did not go to their doctor. Others said they did not have the confidence to tell, whilst a smaller number of women stated that their partner would not allow it.

Over half of the women did see a doctor, but of these only one-third found the GP to be helpful. Most, however, did not tell their GPs about the abuse or denied that it was a problem. Several women were afraid their partners would find out that they had told the GP and where both partners had the same GP, the woman feared for her safety. Clearly when women do tell their GPs this can be a very brave step in their help-seeking process. Some women reported that their GPs were hard to approach and many said that they were not encouraged to talk in busy surgeries. Some women also said that doctors did not ask about the bruising and did not see the obvious signs of injuries. Sometimes GPs would not directly ask about the cause of the injuries but asked instead whether the women had hurt themselves falling down the stairs or walking into furniture. Dobash, Dobash and Cavanagh (1985) refer to this as a process of mutual denial which reinforces the women's view that nothing can be done to help her.

The advice and information given by GPs varied. Whilst some did not see it as part of their job to intervene and a few promised to talk to the husband, the GPs' main response was to prescribe anti-depressants or to pass on the problem to another agency, such as the police, social work and marriage guidance. The advice given by two GPs was to stay in the relationship. In contrast however, some GPs did adopt a more proactive approach to the problem. One of the women referred to a particular GP who had no difficulty in enabling her to issue legal proceedings against her partner. She had become so accustomed to other doctors not saying anything that she was both surprised and delighted when advised to get a solicitor and that a report would be prepared listing the details of her injuries. It was notable that none of the women we interviewed had been referred to refuges or to any of the more specialised services.

We asked the women whether doctors should ask directly about violence and two thirds of the interviewees thought they should. One group of women in a local women's centre suggested that it would be helpful to have one central place dealing with domestic violence where women could consult a doctor who was not their own GP. Women also suggested that doctors should tell their patients about Women's Aid or social workers and spend time talking to the women.

GP Responses

We interviewed nine GPs in the sample areas and identified a range of responses to the problems associated with domestic violence. None of the doctors we spoke to had developed a method for recording cases where domestic violence is a factor. In the absence of this, the GPs were unable to state with any degree of accuracy the exact number of women who had presented with domestic violence on an annual basis. The GPs also acknowledged that they were missing cases and that they themselves often only became aware of the on-going violence when they were requested to produce reports for legal proceedings.

Our study shows that women most frequently attend with the emotional sequelae of domestic violence but that GPs often fail to get to the root of the problem. If a diagnosis does not occur early on then many patients can incur emotional and physical sequalae that may last a lifetime. One GP referred to a patient who had her gall bladder removed before it became apparent that the physical and sexual abuse by her husband was manifesting itself in physical distress. As he said *"at the heels of the hunt, somatization was eventually diagnosed"*.

From our interviews with women who had been physically and sexually abused, we know that they were embarrassed at having to disclose to professionals the details of what has happened to them. Some of the doctors felt that being unable to get appointments with female GPs may discourage some women from seeking help. In our own study, for example, only two out of the nine doctors were women and both worked part-time. The establishment of Well-

Women Clinics in many health centres and surgeries is a useful development and can be used as alternatives if abused women need immediate help.

Several of the GPs we interviewed spoke about their common-sense approach or gut reactions to domestic violence, but acknowledged these were not always sufficient. Some encountered difficulties in placing domestic violence within their professional frame of reference. For example, one doctor described the problems of making a diagnosis if there was no clear physical basis to the symptoms. Some doctors also felt uncomfortable with asking about violence in the home whilst others did not consider it to be their place. In contrast to this, others had introduced ways of providing women with "openers". The need to question patients further about any precipitating factors such as physical or sexual problems was noted by one of the female doctors. When she did this with women who presented with "gynae problems", some of her patients then disclosed the violence in their marriage.

Once domestic violence has been identified, doctors can be reluctant to accept a more widely defined role. One GP, for example, thought that *"his hands were tied"* since it was not a medical problem but more a personal one between the couple. One doctor summarises this more traditional response to domestic violence as *"very delicate territory"* where doctors are unsure of their own particular role. Decisions about whether to offer legal advice or to make referrals outside of the health services, depended for some on their own assessment of how bad the situation was. Some drew a distinction between what they referred to as *"a case of fisticuffs"* and contrasted this to more serious forms of psychopathic violence.

One of the main differences in the various approaches adopted by general practitioners was whether they considered it more appropriate to prescribe medication than to advise on help and support. Most of the doctors felt that anti-depressants should only be used to *"tide the woman over the worst stages"* given the dependency problem and possible side effects associated with such medication. Rather than ending up with a prescription, most of the GPs did believe that patients benefitted much more from time to talk.

However, time was a major factor. GPs felt that their time was constrained by all of the changes that were encroaching on their clinical practice. Echoing other professionals we interviewed, one of the doctors in our study described responding to domestic violence as *"opening the flood-gates"*. There was a general fear that when women did disclose, domestic violence could become very time consuming. For this reason, some GPs passed on the problem to the Community Psychiatric Nurses who they did feel had the time to deal with it. *"Sticking the finger in the dyke"* was how one GP described the medical response to domestic violence. None of the GPs we interviewed had received any training on domestic violence and in the absence of this, some felt they had no clearly defined role. They contrasted this to the response on child abuse where there was much less ambiguity.

What these interviews with both the GPs and the women tell us is that even the doctors who expressed concern about domestic violence were liable to misinterpret the signs. One of the GPs we interviewed, who was particularly concerned about the level of domestic violence in his practice, had in fact not known about two of his own patients who were interviewed for this study. The difficulty is that in the absence of an early diagnosis and lack of accurate recording, women returned to their homes where the violence not only continued, but increased in frequency and intensity. It appeared from both sets of interviews that with the exception of a few doctors, GPs had little knowledge of the more specialised agencies such as Women's Aid or Victim Support.

Accident and Emergency

Given that casualty departments provide emergency services on a twenty four hour basis, it is likely that this would become a major source of help for women who have been subjected to serious assaults. For this reason, we contacted four hospitals in our sample area and interviewed the consultants and senior nursing staff in the accident and emergency departments. Three of these were responsible for major accident and emergency departments while the fourth operated a much smaller unit. Before we turn to their responses, we deal first with the women's experiences of these services.

Women's Experiences

Although women were generally reluctant to get medical help, 39 per cent of women (22) in the survey did go to hospitals for treatment. Ten of these women said they were treated just for their injuries and were not given any advice or information. Even women who disclosed the cause of their injuries after particularly violent attacks did not receive any kind of follow up. One woman found that staff were concerned about her losing her baby (miscarriage) but she felt they should also have been as concerned about the fact that she had been severely beaten.

Several women were able to make up stories or not tell the cause of their injuries and other women reported that they were not asked. One woman who had a head injury had told the staff that she had fallen but thought that it should have been obvious that this was not the case since *"there was a bump here on the top of my head, and a bump there on the back of my head."* Another woman who went to hospitals frequently also made up all sorts of stories and, although she was never challenged or questioned about her stories, she thought the staff must have known. A further problem in her case was that her husband always managed to stay with her in casualty and she thought it would definitely have helped if they had taken him aside.

Not only did the majority of the women believe that the hospital staff should question them more but they gave examples of how to do so. They felt that most women would want to talk and, if approached in a sensitive way, would describe the cause of their injuries. However, the need for immediate advice and information was also raised by several women who thought that staff should definitely tell women who are being abused that there is somewhere to go.

Cynical, uncaring, and too busy attitudes characterised the experiences of a number of women. A woman who was sent by the police to get a checkup for a head injury was given a couple of pain killers and sent home by a doctor who made the assumption that she *"was up for a claim"*. Other women with head injuries were sent home with the men who had assaulted them, despite revealing their predicament to the staff.

Only one woman out of the 22 who attended casualty was referred to a social worker and one was told about Women's Aid. One had a social worker sent to see her. Only three women said they got advice which was critical of the partner and advising them to take action by leaving or charging the partner. In contrast, a sympathetic and supportive approach of the hospital staff was recounted by one interviewee: *"I'll never forget one nurse in particular, I was in shock and I was shaking. She came in and she held my hand and she said where are my children. And she said you're not going back to him, are you . . . The doctor was quite concerned that I would charge him. . . . they did ask if I had somebody to go to"*.

Professional Experience

Four consultants and four senior nurses were interviewed in the casualty departments within our sample areas. Once again, there are problems of recording, identifying and responding effectively to women who have experienced domestic violence. Only one of the four hospitals studied had a data retrieval system but even here domestic violence was not recorded as a separate category. We made further checks on the data to try to obtain the number of assaults in the home which were related to domestic violence. The fact that only two such incidents per month could be found tells us that both the method of recording and the method of identifying domestic violence need to be clarified.

It was evident in these interviews that not all of the staff felt comfortable with identifying, responding to and publicising the problems associated with domestic violence. As some of the staff were aware, they are obviously missing many cases. Insufficient time and lack of awareness of the problem means that staff are not identifying the cause of the problem at an early stage. The need to make an early identification was stressed by consultants who saw a number of patients returning, with the assault being more serious each time. Violence against women can be life-threatening and, if an early diagnosis is not made, the problem can result in more terrifying assaults with very serious and very costly long-term medical consequences.

Passing the problem on was also identified as a specific response in casualty departments. The majority of the staff explained that the clinical notes on the patient are automatically sent to the GP who would be in a better position than them to notice the repetitive nature of the injuries. All four consultants also thought that the nursing staff would have more continuity with the patients, both before and after the medical examination, which would facilitate the development of a rapport and help to establish the cause of the injuries. They also thought that the nursing staff would be in a better position to identify domestic violence than some of the relatively inexperienced junior doctors. However, the nursing staff's views differed on this. One specifically stated that they *"did not get involved with domestic violence"* whilst another thought it was up to the doctors to identify the problem.

Some staff referred to the stigma attached to the statutory social services and women's reluctance to contact social workers, and it appeared that social workers attached to accident and emergency departments were utilised in different ways in the four hospitals. Staff were less reluctant to contact the voluntary services and it is important to note which of these services were prioritised within the accident and emergency departments. The practice differed amongst the hospitals with some giving women the telephone number of the local Women's Aid refuge and others giving out Victim Support leaflets or recommending the Samaritans. Most of the casualty departments had the phone numbers of refuges and some had contacted them directly in the past. Several staff, however, were unsure where the list of refuges and phone numbers were currently located, despite claiming that all new staff were informed of this list at their induction. There were no posters displaying information on domestic violence nor were there any leaflets on Women's Aid in any of the units which we visited.

The nursing staff also referred to the difficulties which they now faced in trying to retain beds for social admissions. Where before they could have kept a woman in overnight, if the violence had been severe and she had wanted some respite from her violent partner, they now have to make decisions about her on medical grounds alone.

Only one of the hospitals had a set of guidelines in relation to domestic violence. This hospital had also adopted procedures on separating the perpetrator from the victim. As with child abuse, they showed that this can be done in a sensitive and, if necessary, imaginative way so that no-one is offended. In the absence of a standard procedure which recognises the need to separate the woman from her violent partner then the opportunity is lost for a woman to disclose what has happened to her – particularly to those in a position to help. It is also important to give the woman both the time and the space where she can safely disclose the cause of her injuries. The need to offer reassurance, advice and appropriate support rather than making a woman feel that she is taking up staff time must also form part of a set of guidelines on domestic violence just as they do on child abuse. The problem of time constraints which the staff have identified needs to be put in proportion to the need to ensure proper treatment and management of the problem. A more pro-active approach would undoubtedly prove to be much more cost-effective. It would also be much more appropriate to the medical principles of diagnosing and addressing the on-going root of the problem.

Suggestions

- *new information leaflets*, designed both for women who do disclose and those who do not

- *widespread dissemination of information*, including leaflets in antenatal clinics and waiting areas and information for ambulance and ancillary staff whom women might approach

- *preparation of a card* with a list of relevant agencies and phone numbers

- *a confidential phone help-line*

- *more liaison with the RUC on new procedures*

- *preparation of a video* to show the quality of a modern refuge

Treatment of Deliberate Self-Harm

Women's Experience

Eight of the women in this study took overdoses or slit their wrists. In the course of telling us their stories they exposed particularly horrific experiences. Most were only treated for physical injuries in hospital and then allowed to go home. There were few referrals and no after care. It was clear to the women that their actions were directly linked to the violence. *"I got that depressed that I took an overdose. I wanted to be dead and I just didn't want to wake up. ...This was the time that these beatings were going on..."* But when they went to hospital, they said they were never asked why they did it and were met with a hostile attitude and aggressive treatment. *"It was the doctor that was on in casualty who was most aggressive. He said, 'it's people like you that waste my time.' I got confused, in the fact that I thought these people were here to help me."*

Telling hospital staff about domestic violence did not guarantee support or after care as one woman experienced. When she was sent to the geriatric ward, she did tell one of the staff about the violence and then slept for several days. *"I just felt secure – he can't get at me"*. But her husband came and put her under pressure to leave the hospital. When the psychiatrist arrived, he spoke to the husband and wife together, so she went home to many more years of violence and several more overdoses.

Professional Experience

Health and social work professionals based in hospitals and in health centres could provide no clear explanation for the number of women who slipped through the net of health and social care after attempted self-harm. In some hospitals women would be admitted to an observation ward attached to casualty where they were likely be seen by a psychiatrist the following day. One hospital consultant felt that most of these para-suicides were *"a cry for help"* and that they needed counselling or advice from a social worker. There was a reluctance to refer them to the psychiatrist since they were not viewed to be *"psychiatrically unbalanced."* Some hospitals mentioned the practice of making *"social admissions"* for women who needed *"time out from the situation"*. However, the number of beds attached to casualty was being reduced and staff were concerned that this particular facility would no longer be an option.

Most social and health professionals agreed that there was a policy that such people should be seen in hospital by the social worker and/ or the psychiatric team and that follow up visits would be arranged as well. But there were different methods used in making referrals and there was no agreement on the success of follow up work.

Health Visitors

Health visitors are in a unique position to provide support for women with children under school age. Since they are a community based service for the healthy population, they have greater access and acceptability to women, and there is less stigma attached to health visitors. Also health visitors regularly visit families after the birth of new babies, a time of stress or crisis for many families and as our interviews have shown, a time of violence for too many women. As most of the women interviewed had young children, it might also be expected that they would have seen a health visitor during the course of the violence.

Women's Experiences

In practice, very few of the women in the sample found they could talk to health visitors about domestic violence and only four of the 25 women who saw health visitors while domestic violence was occurring thought that they had been helpful. Some women did get support. One woman, who spoke to her health visitor before anyone else, said, *"She begged me to leave him and go to my mother. She still asks about me."* But most women said they got no help or advice from the health visitor. When one abused woman took an overdose after she had her last baby and told the health visitor she was depressed, *"She just more or less stated that all women go through this stage of depression after they have had a child, and this was only natural"*.

There were women who thought health visitors should be more understanding of women's feelings and less judgmental when they took partners back. Women particularly looked to health visitors after they had separated and were alone with children. A woman who was afraid she was going to abuse her baby, told the health visitor about her fears and was upset that the health visitor did not return to see her. The women thought health visitors should ask directly or probe about the domestic violence and advise about social workers and Women's Aid. They thought the health visitors should see them more often and for longer; that they should have training about domestic violence and that they should be more aware. One woman said, "A health visitor is one person you are in definite contact with. They should pick up wee signs."

Health Visitors' Responses

Interviews were carried out with 11 health visitors attached to GP practices in the urban and rural sample areas. We also talked to personnel with managerial and training responsibility in this field. Their training teaches health visitors that they are generic visitors for the entire family. But many health visitors have found out that reality is quite different; they are, in practice, providing a woman oriented service. "You are dealing with the woman of the family and around here, the woman is the family." The health visitors interviewed in both rural and urban sectors were therefore concerned to orient their services to the particular needs of the women in their communities. They have been organising mother/toddler groups with meetings and classes, women's groups in rural villages and assertiveness classes in health centres.

Access to women is developed mainly through the long term relationships that are formed in the course of their work with families with children. The health visitors we interviewed were GP attached and in the areas we visited they tend to stay with the same GP and the same families so they get to know the families well. As well as the usual health visiting work, the intensive nature of some new programmes, such as the first parent visiting scheme, provides an opportunity for in-depth work with new mothers.

Health visitors come across domestic violence by knowing the family well, by referrals from GPs, and by women themselves coming in to see the health visitor. They reported that women come with problems such as their own or their children's health, inability to cope with children, financial problems, and family planning. Finding domestic violence, however, is dependent on the level of the health visitor's experience and the nature of her relationship with the woman. One health visitor suggested that, "*If you've known her a long time you usually find that they'd be quite open and quite willing to discuss the fact that domestic violence is taking place. If the relationship is still quite fresh, they are usually very guarded and they are very protective.*" One manager explained that a young health visitor just out of training or coming from a middle class background would have difficulty coping and understanding the problems. However, as the women's interviews have shown, even if the relationship is long-term, domestic violence can still be missed.

The health visitors reported a number of obstacles in the way of helping women. The reluctance of middle class women to disclose violence, the depressive effects of violence which deflates women's ability to change, and women's financial worries were mentioned. "*The biggest problem we feel is money, and if you have a mother and she has been battered herself, but the children are all right, she will say 'well I am living with that man and I may only be £5, £6, £10, better off a week but that will put the food on the table for my children' and they will put themselves through hell*".

Health visitors who were working in rural areas spoke of the particular problems facing rural women and it is important to note that while most of the professionals we spoke to in the rural sector did not consider the issue of domestic violence to be of great importance in that area, the health visitors were concerned about the issue and familiar with a number of cases, both actual and suspect, in their areas of work. They referred to deep-seated problems, such as the severely segregated nature of the family, the conservative influence of the extended family, the general acceptance of violence against women by both men and women in the community and the influence of religion in rural areas.

Agreeing with the views of rural women we interviewed, the health visitors pointed to a number of specific obstacles for women and help providers. There is a lack of services, such as mother and toddler and play groups which would both cater for the needs of children and provide opportunities for women to come together. The lack of housing and local refuges and the heavy pressure on Women's Aid accommodation in other areas has meant that the only alternative for women was bed and breakfast accommodation in a hotel. A health visitor working in a small town said, "*An area like this, there is just no housing. If a woman wants to leave her home, she would have to maybe go to Derry, or away out of the area completely to get a house.*" All agreed on the need for more emergency housing and more refuges in rural areas. The lack of local Housing Executive offices, the poor bus service, and the fact that most of the women do not drive, added to the hardship for women trying to get out of violent relationships.

Resistance to change in rural areas and the constraints imposed on any who raise women-related issues was made clear to health visitors who put up posters or distributed information about domestic violence and found that they immediately "*got the reputation as a very hardened feminist*".

In general, health visitor responses varied with some being rather hesitant about becoming involved and offering advice "*for fear of breaking up the family*", while others were much more proactive in reaching women and providing advice and encouragement. Some health visitors said "*many women expect violence*", but most appeared to be more concerned to respond to the violence and the victim rather than query the causes of the violence.

Some health visitors only offered general advice to women and then referred them to a duty social worker for specific information. Some were reluctant to refer to Women's Aid. However other health visitors carried Women's Aid numbers with them, advised women of all their rights, and have, in the past, escorted women to refuges. Health visitors in one centre had prepared a packet of leaflets with Women's Aid phone numbers and other information about their rights.

Being alert to domestic violence and being the necessary listening ear is of course dependent on the time constraints and pressures placed on the individual health visitor. "*You can only cope with so much of that within your caseload, because you have got other things to deal with. Families at risk. You've kids on the at risk register. Then you've got your ordinary mundane work. There are times that you are so bogged down, and you are so tired, that you are aware yourself, that you are trying to avoid issues".*

Suggestions

In terms of discussing responses to domestic violence, the health visitors described a number of examples of good practice and these are summarised below. In terms of suggestions, these were:

- *more training* on domestic violence

- *development of guidelines*

- *space and facilities for health visitors to provide counselling for women*

- *regular notification of all protection and exclusion orders* issued to women in health visitors' caseloads

Good Practice

1. *Good practice begins with regular meetings between women and health visitors.* Several of the health visitors we talked to pointed out the importance of focusing on women and their needs. "When mothers come to baby clinics, there are things you want to see about the baby. But I think it's important for people just simply to say to them, 'what about you?' Because you can forget about the woman that's behind all this and no matter how liberal we think we are, still at the end of the day, the woman has to bear the brunt of all the crisis."

2. *Getting access to women on their own when violent partners insisted on staying was important to several health visitors when they visited at home.* A high level of commitment was exhibited by this health visitor as she explained, "I just call, call, call and even just carted her out away in the middle of the mountains, so as nobody could get hold of her."

3. *One health visitor emphasised being available for the woman constantly when she is in the midst of deciding to leave her home.* "I would very quickly get them organised. If you see someone has a certain problem, you are going to be calling up, I mean you are not going to be leaving them."

4. *Health visitors have the opportunity to provide follow-up care.* "If I know about it, I would be diligent about seeing that she is all right. Especially if she has young children, I definitely would be there. Sometimes when you go back they are embarrassed about it, and they want to put it in the background, and you just leave it like that. But you do look for wee vibes that you can pick up, that things are starting to go again."

Community Mental Health

Women's Experiences

Five women in our study had been visited by community psychiatric nurses, mostly for treatment for post-natal depression. One woman was not able to talk to the nurse about domestic violence because she thought it was clear that he was there only for the post-natal depression. Another community psychiatric nurse ignored a woman's bruised face. She was on post-natal depression tablets, although she knew that was not her porblem. However, one woman reported the community psychiatric nurse's assistance made an important contribution to her recovery. She had been badly beaten, had a miscarriage, and had not been believed by her family. *"Through talking to him (the CPN), I realised I was a real person."* She thought it was particularly helpful that the visits were in her own home, *"because it wasn't formal. It's not even treatment they give you. It's just a listening ear."* However, another woman thought her decision to stay in a mental health unit to recover from the aftermath of the violence had resulted in her losing custody of her son.

Professional Experience

The response to domestic violence in the mental health field illustrates the dilemma caused by the gap in service provision on this issue. Given that general practitioners are often too busy and social services are either inappropriate or unacceptable, an abused woman can be passed on to a mental health unit. Among mental health professionals there is no consensus about their responsibility for this area of work. One psychiatrist explained that their priority was with people with chronic mental illness and that they cannot take on marital problems as well. With the limited resources available, it was felt that mental health units could not stretch their services to deal with problems such as domestic violence. There is also a more fundamental objection to giving women a psychiatric label because *"it's adding insult to injury, when they are given a psychiatric label, because a man beats them."*

In spite of the labelling, the lack of resources and the possible inappropriateness of the referral, our interviews with mental health teams consisting of psychiatrists, social workers, and community psychiatric nurses (CPNs) in the rural and urban sample areas indicated that domestic violence is an issue for this section of the health service. Our respondents found a reluctance on the part of both general practitioners and psychiatrists to deal with the issue of domestic violence, so referrals were made to social workers and CPNs.

Estimates of 8 per cent to 10 per cent of CPNs' current cases in one area were thought to relate to domestic violence and it was suggested that as many as 30 per cent of new referrals were because of domestic violence. One CPN said that, *"domestic violence is nearly a speciality in itself. You could open up the flood gates, and be inundated with referrals. At the minute, the general practitioners always tell us that they hold back on us. You know, we feel we are flooded at the minute"*.

Domestic violence, however, is never the main presenting issue for a mental health referral. Women would be referred by their doctor because of a range of symptoms such as anxiety attacks, depression, panic attacks, headaches, and inability to sleep. Probing by the CPN often revealed the underlying problem to be marital difficulties and more specifically domestic violence. Recent cases included women who were suffering anxiety attacks because their separated husbands kept coming back into the house and beating them up.

The community psychiatric nurses, known locally as 'nerve nurses', thought that, like the health visitors, they had a greater level of acceptability than social workers in local communities. Coming without uniforms, briefcases, or statutory powers, they thought they were more likely to be seen to be helping, rather than controlling as social workers appear to be viewed. They found that women would talk after they got to know the CPN and they felt they were able to provide the time that is needed in a way that other professions cannot. But the nurses also felt that there was more and more pressure on them to target the major illnesses and said that if Trust status came in, they would have less time for this work. In practice, too, there were different views on the level of proactive responses that should be given. While some nurses said they would advise a woman to leave because they would worry about the violence escalating, others thought they could not encourage her to leave because that would not be counselling.

Suggestions

- Provision of more information for women and in service training on resources for domestic violence.

- A central service or umbrella organisation, not based in social and health services, specialising in domestic violence to provide for all the resources that are now scattered among different agencies.

Alcohol Abuse Units

Women's Experience

Six women were in contact with these units. Most did not find them helpful because of their husbands' refusal to continue the treatment. Several of the men only went to the units in order to placate their partners and did not make any serious effort to reduce their drinking or change their violent behaviour.

Professional Experience

The only unit involved in our study that regularly worked with male abusers and with the women and children who suffered as a result of domestic violence was the alcohol addiction team working in one of the urban areas. This team, which took part in a group interview, is made up of social workers, community addiction nurses and a doctor. The unit had over 900 cases during 1991 and the group estimated that domestic violence is an element in 60 to 70 per cent of their cases. They have had very serious cases with many women going back to violent relationships where they were liable to be killed.

It was emphasised that the programme works with both partners in a relationship. The team works with relatives primarily through the support group that meets in the hospital twice a week. The group thought it was very helpful to the female partners to work in the mixed sex group of relatives. Often the men in the group would be supportive, criticising men's violent behaviour. The team stressed the need to empower women to be able to make decisions for themselves. They thought that it was through the meetings and discussions with the group that women were able to gain confidence. Other members of the group were very important in encouraging the women, making suggestions and persuading them that they were not to blame for the partners' behaviour. The team said they had seen real changes in women's attitudes and behaviour as a result of coming to the group.

The members of this unit said that though they would like to leave decisions to women, sometimes they had to be more proactive. However as with other professional help providers that proactive or challenging position was reserved only for situations in which children, rather than only women, were threatened. Members reported problems because of women's fear of social work intervention; they said this problem was intensified because the alcoholic partner would threaten – *"If you bring the social worker in, they'll take the kids off you."* They have also had the experience of alcoholic fathers using these threats on their children, *"Don't tell anyone because they'll take you away from home"*.

The staff have also found that women's confidence has been eroded as a result of years of living in an abusive relationship. Just as they are blamed for the violence, they have also been blamed by their partners who say *"you make me drink"*. When the staff do confront men about domestic violence, the men deny it or minimise the violence, claiming *"I just slapped her. I only hit her with an open hand, never with my fist"*. The staff agreed that the major motivating factor for admissions to these units was a man's wish to stay with his wife when she was threatening to leave or not take him back. They thought that most were not seriously interested in treatment.

The unit also operates a programme of after-care which includes home visits and support groups in the hospitals and clinics in local health centres. Some of the after-care done by social workers involves the children of these families. For instance they organise day trips for the children whose parents were unable to because of the problems resulting from the alcohol abuse. They have found that often parents would think that the children were not affected or did not know about the domestic violence. But in their discussions with the children, the children would reveal their knowledge.

Suggestions

- *The provision of training* on alcoholism and domestic violence, for staff and for women who, by reacting in the wrong way to an alcoholic, and for example, pouring alcohol down the sink, were liable to get themselves killed.

- *Public education to help overcome the stigma against alcoholism*

- *More community work and after-care support* such as drop in centres in local communities and adolescent centres for alcohol abuse are needed.

- *More staff for preventative work.*

SECTION TWO: OTHER STATUTORY SERVICES

Although this report focuses on the health and social services agencies response to domestic violence, the response of other agencies also affects the context in which they work. Whether or not women can be protected, rehoused and given support impacts on women's decisions and indeed on the responses of the health and social service professions to whom they turn for help. For this reason we have included the civil and criminal justice system and the Housing Executive. These are covered in the same way as above, where women's experiences are included with those of the service providers.

Civil and Criminal Justice

Police

Thirty-five (63 per cent) of the women interviewed contacted the police, almost the same number as contacted housing and social workers. This is a similar level of contact to that found by Montgomery and Bell (1986) but higher than previous research (Evason 1982, Bowker 1983) has found in Northern Ireland and elsewhere. Women from both Catholic and Protestant areas contacted the police either directly about the violence or because of a breach of protection and exclusion orders. There was actually a higher level of contact made by women living in Catholic areas, with 72 per cent (24) of those in our sample making contact compared to 50 per cent (11) of the women living in Protestant communities. This study found that women phoned the police when it was a crisis situation, and most had rung the police more than once while eleven women said they called them often or 'loads' of times.

Although the women often phoned the police, and waited until the situation was particularly critical to do so, only 26 per cent of women found them to be helpful. Similar proportions of Protestant and Catholic women found the police helpful. Those few who gave a positive response thought the police were helpful because the police removed or escorted the male partner from the house. Only three women reported that the police arrested the abuser, and three reported that the police talked to or cautioned the partner and then left. Other positive responses included taking women to a refuge, hospital or relatives. Coming out fast, watching the house, suggesting a solicitor, and getting furniture out were also seen as helpful moves. One woman from Protestant west Belfast had a very positive experience with the police. She praised them highly for the support they had given her and contrasted it with previous experiences she had nine years ago when they had told her that there was *"more serious crime in the area"*. This time, after the introduction of the new police guidelines, when her ex-husband broke in, the police responded immediately and fully supported her when she charged her ex-husband.

Unfortunately most women in the survey group did not have this positive experience, either before or after the introduction of the new force order in 1991. Women reported that police did nothing or wouldn't come out. While this response was reported in many areas of the study, most of the women who reported 'no action' came from west Belfast and other nationalist areas. Women, professionals and the police themselves agreed that there is a slow response time because of the police need to organise security for themselves. However, some women from West Belfast contested the idea that the police should treat their area any differently from others. They argued that the police can be threatened in many different areas so *"why should they insist on coming in here in landrovers, if they come at all, when they go in unmarked cars to other areas."*

Given the research findings that women only phone the police when the violence has become more severe, this lack of police response has serious implications for the women's safety. Not only did several women wait for the police all night, they also reported that they were not even informed that the police were not coming, precluding them from making alternative arrangements for escape. Nor was there any follow up – no one checked up the next day to see if they were still alive. Other women thought the police were too slow, and the abusive partner would get away before the police got there, so they felt phoning them was useless.

Other reasons women thought the police were not helpful, were similar to police responses discussed in other research which found low rates of arrest (Binney 1981), non-intervention (Oppenlander 1982) and attempts to defuse the situation (Parnas 1971). Reports of the police saying that there was *"nothing we can do, it's domestic"*, were described by women in the study in relation to incidents which occurred ten years ago, two years ago and in 1992, after the introduction of guidelines which urge a proactive police response.

Women reported that the police supported the husband or minimised the violence. They found that the police did not believe them and let the partner stay in the house. One woman actually listened on the open phone line as the police took a very conciliatory tone with her ex-husband who had just broken into her house. She heard the police say, *"Look, we have to let her see we're coming over here"*. In other cases, police attempted to conciliate, and offered excuses for the man's behaviour.

As discussed in the women's interviews in Chapter Three, the possession and use of guns was a particularly threatening aspect of domestic violence cases. However when the police were called in, a few women found that the police would not remove their husbands' guns. In one incident when the police did remove the gun from a husband who was a policeman, he was able to retrieve it from the police station the next day.

Shared experiences such as these have deterred many women from counting on the police for assistance. Fear of their husbands was an important reason why several women did not go to the police for assistance. But many others expressed the attitude that the police wouldn't be effective anyway. *"They can't do anything for you unless he sort of knifed you."*

Although we did carry out a number of interviews with police themselves, these are not sufficient to build a composite picture of police response to these serious criticisms.

Protection and Exclusion Orders

The introduction of Protection and Exclusion Orders was a major legal reform to support women by giving them an effective weapon, supported by police and courts, to have a violent partner excluded from their home. Expectations that women can make effective use of these orders are central to the policy of many helping agencies, such as the Housing Executive. Often it is simply assumed that once a woman has a barring order, she is protected because she can go to the police and the courts for enforcement. A full examination of the effectiveness of the Protection and Exclusion orders would require a thorough analysis of the workings of both the police and the civil and criminal justice system, which is beyond the scope of this report. However we can report on the experiences of the women in our survey group and point out some of the problems involved in seeking and using these orders.

Over half of the women (56 per cent) in the study got Protection and Exclusion orders. Reasons given by the other women for not getting these orders included fear of their partners, expected ineffectiveness of the orders, and lack of knowledge. Several women were unaware of their right to get these orders although they had gone to solicitors. We also learned of solicitors who gave erroneous information about the orders.

Only one-quarter of those with orders found them to be useful. Several women found the police reluctant or unsuccessful in finding partners to serve them with the orders. Most women said that even when served, the orders did not offer real protection; husbands ignored them and continued to break into homes, and the orders were not enforced by the police or the courts. An order which had been effective while a woman was in a refuge would become ineffective when she went back into the community. Some who went to court over breaches of the orders found the court response to be merely a small fine and a reprimand.

Other women protested that the orders only applied to the marital home. Under Art. 18 of the Domestic Proceedings (Northern Ireland) Order 1980 courts have the power to apply the exclusion order not only to the marital home, but also to streets and locations such as schools which are in an area contiguous to the home. Indeed, it is possible to have a man excluded from an entire community. However, solicitors interviewed for this project have indicated that the vast majority of exclusion orders apply only to the woman's home and adjoining street. They have argued for reform of the legislation so that courts could designate more than one area and specify particular locations such as schools, the woman's place of work, and relatives' homes which are in different areas from her own home. The interviews with women in this study illustrated that shopping excursions, trips to the school, and journeys to work all became dangerous for women who did not have legal protection in these situations. Awareness of this limitation is essential to understanding the continuous nature of threats to women who leave their violent partners. Often the only safe refuge is for a woman to move to a secret address. But when an order is served, the new address is given on it, informing the violent partner of her new location. Several women said their fear of being found was the reason they did not get exclusion orders. Another problem women found with the orders was the length of time it took, not to grant the orders to women, but to serve them on men. Several women felt they had been endangered because they had moved about without realising that the protection order had not yet been served.

Police and other professionals expressed their frustration because of women's refusals to bring charges against violent partners. However those women who did go to court found it to be a difficult experience and often regretted their decisions. *"It's a terrible hard thing to go in. Even just to get an exclusion order, because you have to convince this judge that you actually need it."* The police, refuge workers and women we interviewed all spoke of the extremely poor conditions of the courts in Northern Ireland with no space for private consultations. *"Everybody can hear your business. You can sit and overhear everything that's happening in somebody's business"*. Women also found it extremely difficult to face their abusers in such close quarters. *"That is the most nerve wracking thing ever. You are scared to get up and go to the toilet, because you don't know whether he is going to put his foot out and trip you, I just sat the whole time, with my head bowed."* Women also felt threatened because they were on their own. *"When he went to the court, he arrived with four or five of his mates . . . I always waited until the court was completely cleared, before I even attempted going out of it. I didn't know that he was going to be waiting round the corner on me."*

For these women the efforts they had to make just did not seem worthwhile both for these reasons and because of the easy access to bail and the leniency of fines or sentences imposed. Women found that not only was there easy access to bail for domestic violence cases, but that bail terms were not enforced by the courts.

Specific suggestions were:

- Women's safety should be considered before granting bail, counselling should be provided for violent partners, and there should be a halfway house where violent partners can live outside of their community and receive counselling while on bail.

- An advocacy system for women could act as a safeguard for women's rights, be a source of advice and information, and provide emotional, and perhaps physical, support in court.

Probation Service

Probation Officers are frequently involved with domestic violence in a wide variety of contexts both in their work with offenders, who can also be the perpetrators of domestic violence, as well as in their work with the families of prisoners. Abused women also need the assistance of probation workers in a variety of contexts.

The few women who were in contact with the Probation Service expressed dissatisfaction because of the concentration of support for their partners and disregard for their own safety. At the time of our study, for example, one woman was in a refuge because of the very bad beatings she received from her boyfriend who was on probation. She was angry that the Probation Officer never came to get a report on that aspect of her partner's activities and resented the support that he appeared to be getting compared to herself.

The women felt that assumptions were sometimes made by those working with offenders that they were willing to have their partners back without prior consultation or without checking first to see if this was the case. They also felt that their security was at risk when an abuser was being released from prison without their knowledge. They suggested some form of contact point for the wives or partners of former prisoners who were known to be responsible for domestic violence and that their safety should be a factor which was central to release planning.

Probation Officers were aware of the complexities of working in this area and felt that the lack of post-custodial care in Northern Ireland compared to England created a gap in their current provision of services. Any threats which women report should also be taken seriously and licence conditions should be constructed with the safety of the victim in mind.

One of the conditions of the Probation Order, states that the offender *"be of good behaviour and lead an industrious life"*. If an assault which constitutes grievous bodily harm has been shown to have taken place, then an offender may be returned to court for having breached the Order. Probation Officers were aware that an assault by the man on his partner was technically such a breach but, in practice, it was rarely the case that domestic violence was perceived as constituting such grounds. Concern was expressed by one of the Probation Officers that this condition can be interpreted in different ways and may indeed lead to allegations of collusion between the perpetrators of domestic violence and the Probation Service or to accusations that staff are not treating domestic violence as seriously as other forms of violence.

One of the probation workers we interviewed had introduced some methods of working with a client who was on probation for an offence which was not related to domestic violence. The purpose of this work was to ensure that the man accepted responsibility for his violent behaviour and to examine controls which might prevent further violence. A Probation Officer involved with the Prison Link service affirmed the complexities of responding to the needs of offenders whilst being alert to the needs of the victim where domestic violence was concerned. This Probation Officer noted that, in cases where men who are on remand in custody request to see their partners, it was important to consider the offence which they have been charged with in order to avoid any collusion with the alleged offender. Situations can arise where men use the visits to put pressure on their partners to withdraw their cooperation with the prosecution process.

In Northern Ireland, as elsewhere, Probation Officers were aware that a good deal of controversy existed over judicial decisions to divert from prison which were too often taken for reasons that did not acknowledge the seriousness of the offence, treated it as a family matter, and/or did not recognise the need to offer protection to the victim. The Association of Chief Probation Officers had adopted a position paper on domestic violence which formed the basis of good practice in this field.

Housing

The provision of temporary accommodation and access to rehousing has been a crucial development in the long struggle to support women victims of domestic violence. The knowledge that they can get a home in their own name has helped many women to leave violent relationships or to have greater control if they decide to stay with their partners. The new legislation on homelessness, the Housing (NI) Order 1988, recognises domestic violence, for the first time in Northern Ireland, as the basis for priority housing. Since the legislation became effective in 1989, the responsibility for housing women who leave violent partners has shifted from social services to the Housing Executive. As a result the Housing Executive is increasingly becoming the first, and for some, the most important contact for women looking for help. This study confirms reports that the available resources, the provisions in the legislation, the policies under which it operates, and the procedures and attitudes that women face in local housing offices have an important effect on women's ability both to leave and to stay away from violent partners (Victim Support 1992).

Women's Experiences

Fifteen of the 36 women who went to the Housing Executive found them to be helpful. These included women who obtained temporary accommodation, who were rehoused and who received advice and sympathetic attitudes when they went to the housing office. However the women's experiences also indicate a number of problems with the housing legislation, policies and procedures.

Women had to verify that there had been actual or threatened physical violence to be accepted as unintentionally homeless and they often found they were not believed. If women came in with bruises or other injuries, there was no problem but those who had no obvious injuries or professional evidence faced long delays or refusals. The women also had to prove that they were serious about leaving their partners by, for example, producing separation orders. They felt in addition that they were pressurised to make immediate decisions when they had not yet had time to seriously consider their options.

Women who had previously been allocated new houses and then taken partners back had particular difficulty in becoming accepted as unintentionally homeless when they left again. One woman felt that *"The Housing Executive don't understand that it is hard to actually leave the husband because of the fear and the threats that you undergo if you do leave"*. One woman whose violent husband has managed to find her and break into her house many times has been refused housing in the area where her family is living. She reports that the housing officer told her *"you're not getting back in here. I don't want you on my housing list."*

The women reported pressure on them to stay in the marital home. There was a policy, confirmed by Housing Executive personnel, to attempt to move the man rather than women and children. This policy appeared to be particularly applied to women coming from owner occupied housing. But many women thought it would not be safe to move back into the marital home. *"I wanted a house where he wouldn't know where I was."* Others did not want to live in the house where they had had such terrible experiences. This Housing Executive policy is based on the presumption that the women can get Protection and Exclusion orders and that they will be effective. *"He says the way we look at it you have a house, and if you have a protection order and an exclusion order, if your husband comes, you can call the police"*.

Women objected to having to tell their story over and over again to strangers. In the attempt to get rehoused, they found they might have to go to two or three housing centres if they were moving out of their own area. It would be more helpful, they said, to have one central office with the women's files on record rather than for women to go to different offices.

The high demand for temporary housing and the lack of accommodation in Women's Aid refuges has meant many abused women and children are placed in hotels, guest houses or bed and breakfasts which are unsuitable for their needs. There is a potential risk to women and children if this short-stay housing is also used to accommodate men who have been released from prison following conviction for Schedule 1 offences (cited in McGibbon, Cooper and Kelly 1990). Women from both rural areas and towns were placed in this type of accommodation and several told us they had gone back home rather than accept it. One woman explained, *"It was a bed and breakfast, and there was me and the three children in one wee room away at the top of an attic, and it was freezing and it was damp, and there was millions of flies in it, and it was windy and rainy, and I had no money, and we used to walk down to the Water Works, and the kids were all foundered …here's me okay, come on, I'll take you home."* Such experiences are a strong argument for the provision of more resources for temporary accommodation.

Several of the women in the survey stayed in Housing Executive managed hostel accommodation. But some reported that their husbands found out where they were, although the Housing Executive personnel have told us it is not practice to divulge the women's whereabouts. In the hostels there is not the same sense of solidarity and shared awareness of danger among the residents as is found in women's refuges.

The stress on the women as they waited to get permanent housing also took its toll. We met several women whose resolve was weakening because it took so long to be rehoused. One woman *"felt forgotten"* after four weeks. But to be rehoused in areas of high demand like West Belfast, women might have to wait for up to six months. Other women thought they were being pressurised into taking unacceptable housing or 'bad' areas.

Housing Executive Response

We interviewed a number of housing managers, housing officers and hostel wardens in the survey areas and found variations in the perceived prevalence of the issue in the different areas. Most of those interviewed said that women claiming domestic violence in the initial assessment were generally accepted as unintentionally homeless. "It is one of the most difficult areas, and it is one where generally we would err on the side of caution." But verification from social workers, doctors, or court orders might be necessary in some cases. Statistics centrally collected by the Housing Executive show that the majority (65 per cent) of those presenting with domestic violence are accepted as unintentionally homeless. This is much higher than the overall average of 41 per cent of cases that are accepted. The lack of effectiveness of Protection and Exclusion Orders and the lack of police support in many areas was acknowledged by most housing personnel interviewed.

The temporary accommodation available to women includes Women's Aid and other refuges which are reserved for women and children who have been victims of domestic violence, Housing Executive hostels for homeless persons, and bed and breakfast and hotel accommodation arranged by the Executive. The refuges are organised on the basis of communal living, provide social and emotional support for women and children, and have professionally trained staff who have experience in dealing with the issue of domestic violence.

The Housing Executive hostels provide excellent fully furnished individual flats in a number of locations. Wardens pointed out that since there are no communal facilities, residents do not regularly get to know each other. While there is a warden on 24 hour duty, they have no particular training in domestic violence. While many of them voluntarily serve as advisors and supporters of women in the accommodation, this is not part of their job description and the Housing Executive has not considered it necessary to provide training for them. Also the privatised design of some of the flats results in less easy access to the warden and less security for the women.

There was variation in the methods used by housing officers in assigning temporary accommodation. In some offices all of the options were explained to the women and the choice, depending on bed space, was left up to them. Other officers recommended Women's Aid to those who were thought to be in need of particular support, while others used only their own list of accommodation, perhaps reflecting their personal antipathy towards Women's Aid. For example, one senior housing manager said, *"Women's Aid is not suitable for some women"* and *"women would not want to go there anyway"*.

Both housing officers and Women's Aid staff have referred to problems resulting from the pressure on women to make immediate decisions on their relationships and on housing. Women's Aid staff felt that the seven day period for assessing a woman's housing status does not allow sufficient time for a woman to make reliable decisions about her future housing options. There was also concern that a woman in crisis should not have to proceed to court as proof of her decision to leave a violent relationship.

It has been the experience of housing officers that most women want and need to resettle near their families after marital breakdown. This need presents difficulties, particularly in areas of high demand, with three months the earliest that women could expect to be rehoused. Other women who choose to move to a totally new area may end up feeling isolated and want to come back to their original community. But it is very hard for these women to come back once they have accepted another tenancy.

The problems of rehousing have been accentuated by the government policy of selling off Housing Executive housing stock. In one sample area the local housing manager pointed out that very few people are being rehoused because around a third of the housing stock has been sold off and is therefore not available to the Housing Executive for letting. Since this stock has been reduced, there is increased pressure on women to take unacceptable housing.

The pressure on rehousing has meant long stays in temporary accommodation for many. Some in our study were in a refuge for up to a year. Other research (McGibbon 1989) indicates that over three months is too long for women to stay in a refuge. Women have already received the necessary initial support and they are taking up space needed by others in crisis situations. The Housing Executive has recognised this need in their review (NIHE 1992) indicating that there is a *"general shortage of supported self-contained accommodation for vulnerable lone parents, some of whom need a 'half-way-house' after leaving hostel accommodation"*. This review has recognised women at risk of domestic violence as a particular group in need of accommodation and acknowledges the need for more provision.

Conclusions

The interviews with the majority of the statutory agencies reveal an absence of guidelines and of any clear-cut recording of domestic violence. There was no specialisation within the professions and it was apparent that a lack of continuity in practice existed with the result that women could easily be simply passed from one service provider to the next. However, they also appeared frustrated and were unsure of their professional responsibility within this field of work. They were particularly anxious that domestic violence was becoming one more problem in an already busy and overloaded schedule. It was immediately apparent that there was an absence of training on domestic violence for all professional groups. The issue had not been included in either pre- or post-qualification education. Nor indeed was it being picked up on any of the in-service training courses these groups had attended. The subject of child abuse has become an integral part of professional education and training. Occasionally domestic violence may be subsumed within this curriculum. It is not, however, sufficient to deal with domestic violence in this way, as it is a separate issue and requires an alternative approach in its own right. Some professionals had good practice ideas and made suggestions for improvements which could well be taken up in training which needs to be developed.

The interviews with the medical and health professionals showed how the violence could often be minimised and not diagnosed or identified. The problem here was that the violence, if not dealt with at an early stage, could result in more terrifying assaults with very serious long-term medical and social consequences. The interviews with social workers indicated that the lack of statutory responsibility, the divisions of functions within the profession, attitudes about domestic violence, lack of training and resources, and a fear of being overwhelmed by the issue, were among the factors that produced a reluctance to use the resources of social services to tackle the issue of domestic violence.

There was much variation of approach among the professionals interviewed for this study. Some adopted a sympathetic response to the problem by allowing women, what they frequently called, *"the opportunity to ventilate."* Women do want to be listened to, to be believed and not blamed, but we have to question how positive a response this is when it does not reach beyond sympathy to provide a more challenging response to the problem. Other professionals appeared to be more willing to ask directly about the cause of the injuries and had developed a number of techniques which enabled abused women to feel more comfortable in disclosing. Those dealing with the "healthy" population were in a good position to provide services for women when they did disclose about the violence.

Analogies were frequently drawn with the policy and guidelines which had been introduced to deal with child abuse. However, professionals differed in the extent to which they thought these were necessary and were concerned about limits to flexibility. There was a lack of consensus about the need for intervention, given that some professionals felt that women were adults and could make up their own minds. They found no difficulty in adopting a more proactive approach to their work when concerns for children's welfare were being expressed. As we found in our interviews with women, however, years of abuse can also erode a woman's ability to make effective decisions. When women did get advice and information, they were often then enabled to take the next step. In the absence of information and advice, many of the women we spoke to did not know what their rights were and could not therefore effect change in their own lives.

Responses were also coloured by traditional beliefs that value the maintenance of the family and reinforce the subordinate position of women within it. The danger of adopting this response is that the abuse is seen as the woman's problem rather than that of her partner. Some services have been developed which operate in an empowering way to challenge these assumptions, but it appeared that the more specialised services of agencies such as Women's Aid were not drawn upon even when the violence had been identified. One can only speculate on the extent to which this reflected the attitudes of the professionals or revealed the lack of detailed knowledge about the work of these voluntary agencies.

The lack of liaison with professionals outside one's own field is one of the major problems currently identified and the need for a multi-disciplinary working party is something on which all staff were agreed. Not intervening at an early stage, with either the victim or the perpetrator of domestic violence can have implications for the different service providers as they begin to encounter the manifestation of the problem in a variety of medical, psychiatric, health and social service settings. Not following up on cases where there has been evidence of serious assaults can also lead to women believing that nothing can be done. This is the process which results in a double victimisation of women, once by the perpetrator and then again by the system to whom she turned for help.

FIVE

The Voluntary Sector

Voluntary sector provision in any area is, at its best, about initiating developments, filling gaps, raising issues and providing an alternative, and occasionally, more specialised range of services. And, at its worst, an unstable and 'cutting corners' substitute for statutorily provided services. In the case of domestic violence, there are many agencies which in principle can be involved when women seek help for the multitude of problems facing them. This chapter discusses the experiences of a few of these organisations, including Marriage Guidance agencies, the Samaritans and Women's Centres. The main focus of the chapter, however, is on Women's Aid, since this agency is central to the provision of services on domestic violence and indeed first raised the issue as far back as 1975. We also include the comments of one other refuge provider, given that women in our sample also went there for help. As in the last chapter, we cover both the experiences of the women and the responses of the staff.

Women's Aid

Women's Aid is the main agency providing refuge and support for women and children experiencing domestic violence in Northern Ireland. The organisation not only provides emergency accommodation through its network of refuges but has also developed considerable expertise in the provision of advice, information and support. The first permanent refuge was opened by Belfast Women's Aid in 1978, and since then eight other refuges have been established. Funding for these was initially secured through the various Health and Social Services Boards but following legislation on homelessness, in 1989, the Northern Ireland Housing Executive has also become responsible for the financial support of the refuges.

The Northern Ireland Women's Aid Federation, similar to the Federations in England, Scotland and Wales, has a range of functions. These include acting as the co-ordinating body for the ref uges; liaising with other statutory and voluntary agencies; and undertaking research and collating information on domestic violence. Functions also include providing information and training for professionals working in the field; fund-raising and mobilizing resources for advice and support work; and lobbying for legislative change and raising public awareness on domestic violence.

Dobash, Dobash and Cavanagh (1985) show that few public agencies are prepared directly to assist the woman whilst at the same time challenging male violence and dominance. Women's Aid state that they have a deliberate philosophy which both supports women and challenges the attitudes and behaviour of those who perpetrate the abuse. Their principles can be summarised as follows:

[a] that the abused woman's perspective is of central importance in the provision of support and services;

[b] that self-help and mutual support are the most appropriate methods of assisting abused women and their children;

[c] that children's emotional, developmental and educational needs should be addressed;

[d] that women should be enabled to regain control over their own lives and that they should be empowered to make decisions in a non-judgemental way;

[e] that changing social attitudes by effectively challenging assumptions about male dominance and control is the key to freeing society from the misery which results from abusive relationships.

The organisation has an open door policy and, unlike other agencies, does not seek proof of the abuse which the woman has experienced. In 1991/92, the organisation provided accommodation for 587 women and 1,034 children in Northern Ireland. The majority of women (70 per cent), stayed approximately two weeks. For others, however, there was a more prolonged stay, with 16 per cent of women remaining up to two months and 13 per cent staying for four or more months. Difficulties can arise when a refuge is full, but in the case of self-referrals, the staff use their network of workers to try to locate accommodation elsewhere in one of their refuges.

However, given the lack of accommodation that still prevails, the refuges were unable to accommodate 474 women and 1,094 children in 1991/92. One of the major concerns for Women's Aid is the use of unsuitable accommodation on a relatively frequent basis, mainly outside of the urban areas. The Coordinator of Women's Aid has targeted a number of regions in Northern Ireland where there are no refuges currently and where these difficulties are particularly acute.

Women's Experiences of Refuges

Refuges can be many things for many women. They can be the place where women recover from their shame and isolation and where they gain support, help and friendship. They enable many women to make decisions with regard to their relationships and they can be a turning point for a large number of women. Over half (57 per cent) the women in the sample were currently in or had previously been to a women's refuge. A few had been to Sydenham House and others had been to refuges in England, but most had gone to Northern Ireland Women's Aid. This was the one service with which women expressed high levels of satisfaction. Two-thirds were satisfied, despite the communal living arrangements and occasional overcrowding.

Some of the women we interviewed felt that for them coming to a refuge was a last resort, particularly if they associated it with an inferior standard of accommodation. They spoke of their surprise on arriving, to find such a high level of facilities in the refuge. Safety was the key reason why these women thought the refuge was helpful. Equal prominence was given to assistance in contacting solicitors and other agencies and to the support that children received in the refuge. The women spoke of the services for their children which ranged from supervised play and educational sessions to a variety of activities and outings in the evenings and at weekends. They were able to use this time, unencumbered by children, to make telephone calls, to visit their solicitor or local social security agency and to share their experiences and information with other women in the refuge. The facilities were, therefore, of mutual benefit to both the women and children.

One woman described how she felt overcome with the help she received when she first arrived and several women discussed the changes which had taken place in themselves because of their stay in the refuge. One woman Traveller indicated that Women's Aid always gave her space and for some women, this was all they wanted. For others however, the increased confidence and self-assurance gained from being in a refuge enabled them to build their lives again and to come to terms with having to cope alone. One woman described this kind of healing process by saying: *"I do get it out of my system . . . you know you are not the only one it has happened to. It has actually happened to lots of others."*

Several women discussed their first reactions, and how they blamed themselves for being in the refuge. Such feelings did not appear to last long in the refuge with women recalling that they soon felt at ease, as if they were at home. Those women who were negative about their stay in a refuge reported that they were not able to settle into the communal living or were not able to get along with the other women. Even those who thought the refuge was wonderful, pointed to the lack of privacy as a drawback and felt a sense of loss at not being in their own homes.

In the group interviews in refuges and in interviews in the community, many women said they had never heard of Women's Aid or refuges until they needed help this last time. Others had vaguely heard of refuges, but would not have known how to make contact. A few women told us about the very circuitous help seeking process they went through before they found Women's Aid. The lack of knowledge about refuges and the difficult task that many women had in finding out about Women's Aid indicates the need for the provision of more and better information about women's refuges. Several women suggested that TV advertising campaigns were needed.

However, we found that the lack of information about refuges was not the only factor limiting women's use of refuges. Many of the women, some of whom were still in violent relationships, knew about refuges but would not use them. When we asked "Would you have left sooner if you had known about refuges?" more women (15) said they would not than the women who said they would (10). Most who gave negative replies explained that they had family support to fall back on. Several women however referred to a stigma about being in refuges and, by implication, about being a "battered woman". Other women thought that their life would be too disrupted in a refuge, whilst still others referred to specific problems such as the Women's Aid rule against taking boys over the age of 15. Having to leave their older sons behind was one of the problems faced by Traveller women who had larger families. Having to return to their older sons, also meant that they were more likely to go back to the violence. The unavailability of refuges for mothers of adolescent boys remains a problem to be addressed.

Response of Refuge and Federation Staff

We interviewed eleven staff from Women's Aid. Of these, eight worked in refuges, one of whom was a childcare worker. The others included the Regional Coordinator, an advice centre worker and a volunteer who currently works in the Federation. As we have noted, Women's Aid holds the view that a belief in women themselves to effect change in their lives should underpin all that happens in a refuge. Staff thus stressed that women are encouraged to take part in house meetings, to help other women to settle in and to be involved in the day to day running of the refuge. As one of the workers noted *"we want each woman to feel that this is her home and that she can share in the decisions that are made."* Using a system of support groups attached to each refuge, women are encouraged to return as volunteers so that their experience and skills can be drawn on by other women.

Refuge workers also work therapeutically with children and provide assistance in dealing with bureaucracy. One of the childcare workers believed that if an understanding of what the children were going through was addressed in the refuges, then the coping strategies of the children could be developed, alongside that of the mothers.

The provision of a safe haven for women is of central importance and to ensure women's security, Women's Aid have adopted the practice of not allowing male partners access to refuges. This has been open to criticism in the past; however as a result of media attention on recent attacks on women from their former partners, the need for maximum security is now recognised by those outside the organisation. Rather than being the subject of criticism, the high profile attached to security and the guidelines which the organisation has developed to protect a woman constitute good practice in this field. An additional feature of this policy which was pointed out to us by one of the refuge workers and which should be taken into consideration in the context of the culture from which the women come, is that it enables women to return home without any recriminations from their male partners about mixing with other men.

The staff we interviewed also discussed the particular problems experienced by Travellers whilst they were living in the refuge. Problems can arise in ensuring the safety of Travellers' children since they are particularly vulnerable to being abducted by relatives. It has to be added that this situation also arises for many women and children in refuges, but what makes it distinctive for Travellers is their highly developed communication network and the codes of honour which are specific to their culture. These make it difficult for women to keep their place of refuge secret, even from other women in their community. Occasionally, the stereotypes which exist amongst women can be accentuated when Travellers and women from the settled community are living together in the same refuge, but the workers recognised that a refuge can also be the setting in which to break down some of the prejudice which exists.

Referrals and liaison featured in discussions with staff. According to 1991/92 figures from Women's Aid, the majority of women (42 per cent) who make contact with the refuge are self-referrals. Women also find out about Women's Aid from friends or relatives (6 per cent) or organisations such as the Samaritans (5 per cent). Consistent with our own data on service providers, a significantly small proportion of women (1 per cent) are referred by GPs and hospitals. Referrals also come from agencies such as the social services (18 per cent), the police (6 per cent), and the Housing Executive (10 per cent). Given the recent changes to the housing legislation it is surprising that only one out of every ten women comes to Women's Aid through the Housing Executive. This may be a reflection of the way in which the figures are currently collated. It may also be the result of an internal policy of the Housing Executive, as discussed above, to refer women to other types of accommodation, particularly where they have developed their own specialist accommodation and are anxious to assign women to these "homeless units".

If there are concerns over the welfare of the children then referrals can be made, with the woman's knowledge, to the social workers or health visitors attached to the refuges. Refuge workers emphasise that the liaison with the various statutory agencies attached to the refuges has been developed over the years and is now working very effectively. They remained concerned however about the problems which women encounter when they are passed from one agency to the other. One initiative to counteract these problems is the establishment of an interagency forum on domestic violence in Newtownabbey with which Women's Aid are currently working (See Annex 4).

Despite the training which had been carried out by the organisation over recent years, there was a general view that the requests from health and social service professionals working in the Universities or in the statutory sector come as a result of personal contacts rather than being a central part of the educational curriculum. Social work staff in the local universities have obtained placements in refuges which have proven to be beneficial to the students. Requests to facilitate in-service training courses are less extensive than they perhaps should be, particularly in the light of recent legislative changes in this area. Only one multi-disciplinary training programme had requested the participation of Women's Aid staff alongside a team of medical and health professionals. This had proved to be a productive exercise which, it was felt, could serve as a useful model for others.

Good Practice and Suggestions

In one of the rural areas, a refuge worker referred to a recent innovation where a member of staff from the Citizen's Advice Bureau in a neighbouring town had spent a week in the refuge familarising herself with the work of Women's Aid. This enabled the staff in the advice centre to offer a higher level of support to women who sought their help on domestic violence. This was a particularly effective approach, as the refuge was the only facility in this large rural area and it was difficult to reach women in any other way. Enabling women, who are thinking of getting out of a violent relationship, to visit the refuge beforehand was also suggested as a way of overcoming the fear which women experience in leaving home.

Staff in the Federation also identified the need for a help-line which could be used by women who cannot easily gain access to a local refuge or women wishing to seek help whilst remaining anonymous. They had recently begun to develop such a resource which enabled these women and women living in rural areas to receive the kind of support which women have in refuges. This counselling service was also identified to meet the needs of women who were experiencing abuse but did not intend ending the relationship.

Aftercare and resettlement work for women who had left the refuge was also identified as an area of need. A note of caution was added, however, that such services required a considerable increase in resources to provide the necessary back-up facilities.

Other Refuge Providers

Outside of Women's Aid, there is one other refuge facility available which offers accommodation specifically to abused women and their children. This is known as Sydenham House and is located in east Belfast. It offers a place of respite for women.

While emphasising that they were not trained counsellors, the staff in this refuge also support women who have made a decision to end the relationship. They were concerned that the housing choices for some women had recently become more limited and referred to the level of discretion which appeared to exist in the housing offers made to women in the refuge. They felt that more training was needed for professionals working in this field and recommended a multi-disciplinary working party to sort out some of these problems.

Aftercare for women who had left the refuge was also highlighted as a particular gap in their current services. The refuge worker in Sydenham House recommended that financial provision should be made to facilitate the installation of a telephone in the woman's new home in order to ensure her security on leaving the refuge.

What, then is the overall impact of the refuges? Women, as we have seen, by and large respond positively to the philosophy that underpins refuge provision, and, though some have reservations, appreciate the services and facilities which are on offer, not only for themselves but for their children. Staff, however, feel constantly under pressure due to a lack of resources and are aware that further funding is required for future development.

In outcome terms, approximately half of the women who come to these refuges do return to their partners, although, according to one worker *"each time women go back, they are a bit stronger."* In the absence of research, however, we can only speculate on the effects of refuges on abusive relationships. Pahl's (1978) longitudinal study, for example, showed that very few women who had entered refuges returned permanently to their husbands but that many of these women had returned in the short-term before making the final decision to leave. A more recent study suggests that the beneficial effects of shelters might be dependant on the attributes of the victim (Berk, Newton and Berk 1986). If the woman is seen as actively taking control of her life, a refuge stay may dramatically reduce the likelihood of further abuse, but in other situations, the refuge may have little or no impact. Further research is needed in Northern Ireland to assess the long-term impact of refuges, particularly given the context of the specific culture from which the women come.

We move on now to discuss the other agencies to which the women in the sample turned for help. We discuss briefly and in turn, marriage guidance agencies, women's organisations, the Samaritans and Al-Anon and Alcoholics Anonymous.

Marriage Guidance Agencies

Thirteen women reported that they contacted marriage guidance agencies. This was a larger number than used any other voluntary organisation with the exception of Women's Aid. The chance to talk separately from their partners, the support in getting their point across to their partners and the fact that they were not encouraged to stay in the relationship were reported as positive aspects of the contacts. Some women were greatly encouraged by the confidence they gained and the support they were given in coming to understand that the violence was not their fault. On a more negative note, problems raised were partners' failure to go to meetings or to treat meetings seriously, and the long waiting lists for appointments.

Several women went to marriage guidance for help with separation and problems with access to children thereafter. While these contacts were, on the whole, helpful, there were difficulties. One woman felt that the agency acted as an *"information service"* for her husband because it let her violent ex-husband know her exact whereabouts in the process of improving his access to the children. From the woman's point of view this endangered herself and her children and she had to change her schedule and keep her movements hidden.

Interviews conducted with representatives of the two major marriage guidance agencies, Relate – Northern Ireland Marriage Guidance and the Catholic Marriage Advisory Council, indicated that domestic violence is indeed a relevant factor in the work of these agencies. One organisation thought it occurred in about 20 per cent of their cases while the other thought it was *"one of the most common problems"*. Relate has developed special procedures to ensure the safety of women when both partners are meeting for counselling or mediation.

Their experience indicates that the continued stigma against divorce, particularly for women in Northern Ireland, has deterred women from leaving violent relationships. They also found that women's fears kept them in violent relationships. These included the fear of being alone, making decisions, lack of money, but also women's fears that they would be thought of as "bad women" if they left first. It was suggested that there were particular problems facing middle class women who left the marital home because of domestic violence because, through no fault of their own, they would lose their home and their standard of living.

In responding to domestic violence, one person indicated that *"the one message that they would very clearly get, is that the pattern of violence, from one to the other is unacceptable"*, but there appeared to be considerable stress placed on shared responsibility for the violence, rather than acceptance of the unilinear nature of violence from male to female. In counselling they would try to enable the couple to understand what were the causes of the violence, asking *"Is there some sort of trigger?"* When counselling did not work or a counsellor thought there was physical danger, then responses to women still involved in violent relationships became challenging, *"well why are you staying in this marriage?"*

Interviewees made a number of suggestions:

- education is necessary to raise the self-esteem of women and men. (Relate has an education training team which goes out to schools and works in the area of relationships and sexuality with teenagers, as well as in-service work with teachers.)

- counselling provision is needed for violent partners

- support and understanding for women and for children coming out of violent relationships is crucial.

Women's Organisations

Women's centres and organisations in the sample areas were visited and representatives were interviewed about their experiences on the issue of domestic violence. While some of the newer women's centres showed some reluctance openly to discuss domestic violence, the longer established centres have regularly dealt with the issue and have developed impressive expertise. In rural areas, however, it is more difficult to raise any women-related issues. One rural worker explained that she had to be very careful when talking about women's groups in her area because *"this society is not ready for those kind of issues and does not necessarily want to recognise them"*.

A number of women's voluntary organisations, both 'general' women's centres, and specialised services such as Rape and Incest Line and Rape Crisis Centre, put forward the argument that they are providing specialised services for women which cannot be supplied by general advice organisations. They argue that community based women's centres offer a holistic service for women, and have positive advantages in their provision of both practical and emotional support. A woman can, for example, attend assertiveness classes or use a drop-in facility in a women's centre without any necessary assumption that she has a 'problem', and can receive advice, counselling and/or practical help as a 'user' not a 'client'. She can also disclose abuse when she is ready and can receive support over an extended period in an informal setting. Women's voluntary groups also argue that they can provide a professional service where it is possible for the user to feel that the service providers are her peers rather than social service professionals who can carry a stigma in local communities.

Some women are reluctant to approach an agency outside their own area. Both the Falls and Windsor Centres referred to this problem. One centre that has developed expertise on the issue of domestic violence is the Falls Women's Centre. Women who come to this centre are drawn from all over Northern Ireland as well as the local area. During the year 1991/92, the centre dealt with 140 cases of violent assault, the majority of which were the result of domestic violence. There was severe criticism of the quality of statutory provision available for women. As well as providing advice and making referrals if necessary, centre workers organise solicitors for women and accompany them on visits to doctors, and hospitals, as well as to any court hearings that occur. They have found that not only is this helpful to women, but it also puts positive pressure on professionals. *"If somebody is sitting in the waiting room, they'll appreciate that there is a serious problem"*.

A more specialised service is provided by The Rape Crisis Centre which offers telephone and personal counselling and support to women who have been sexually abused. The centre gets many cases of domestic violence in which a woman has been beaten and raped by her husband or partner. They thought that marital rape was *"fairly common"*, though they find women extremely reluctant to disclose this abuse. In some of their cases, domestic violence is combined with the abuse of children in the family. RCC workers were concerned about the gaps in provision for women, such as the need for a special refuge for women who have been raped. It was also argued that although social services have a statutory responsibility for children up to the age of 18, *"there are far too many young people falling through the net. These children have problems with violence at home and end up on the streets where they fall prey to glue sniffing, alcoholism and prostitution"*.

Centre workers had a number of suggestions:

- *"Don't expect women suddenly to make decisions to change the course of their lives"*. (Centre workers have found that if violence is going on for a long time, women's decision making capacity is severely reduced.)

- Women need confidence and assertiveness, but more importantly they need a whole infrastructure of support from all the public officials and others who deal with women.

- There is a need for greater awareness and the provision of training for the full range of professionals from solicitors, judges and probation officers to doctors and social workers.

- More flexibile and extensive powers in Protection and Exclusion Orders are necessary. *"It's an important first step, to go and see a solicitor, to get a Protection Order, to come to terms with it, to assert yourself"*.

- There is a need for refuge provision for younger women, aged 16 to 19, who have left their families or have left care because of violence and abuse.

- A local independent centre which could provide a range of services including an independent doctor, a counselling service and an advocacy system which would support women in court hearings should be established. Such a centre should still receive recognition and cooperation from social services and the police.

Samaritans

The Samaritans are well known for their 24 hour telephone help line for people who feel suicidal or depressed. But the organisation also operates a counselling centre staffed by trained volunteers enabling people to drop in during the day or evening for personal sessions.

The six women in our survey who went to Samaritans thought they were helpful mostly because there was someone to listen, and because they were there anytime. However, others, while agreeing that it was helpful to talk, said they wanted more than listening. *"I want someone to say it's wrong."* Some phoned Samaritans expecting information and advice and while a few did get information about Women's Aid and advice to leave their partner, others expressed disappointment that they got no advice.

Staff stated that abused women come to the Samaritans very often, although violence is usually not the presenting issue. A Samaritan volunteer explained that while depression would be the most common problem presented, a woman may phone up and talk about other things such as her inability to pay the bills, and domestic violence will be hidden among a host of other problems. Experience has shown that women are often reluctant to disclose violence because of the negative reactions they have had before from families and other agencies. The Samaritans get the full spectrum of women who are in abusive relationships – those just starting out, those in short term relationships, and women who have been married to violent men for 30 to 40 years. Women also come with different experiences of help seeking. For some it is the first time they ever disclosed the violence. But others have tried everything and at the end of the cycle of help still find that the original problem has not been addressed. One volunteer found that quite often *"they feel that they have been tricked by agencies or professionals, who were going to help them, but didn't"*.

The Samaritans' response is based on providing a confidential non-directive service. The philosophy of the organisation is *"to help people find their own solutions"*. A volunteer explained that while they would explore possibilities with the woman, they would avoid making any judgements or specific suggestions because that would be adding to the pressures already on her. Security, time and respect were thought to be key issues in supporting abused women. It was also pointed out that support often takes time, and abused women might need support for years before an effective solution is found. Experience has shown that abused women are *"totally degraded by years of abuse"* and they are often *"not well placed to make any sort of rational decision"*. The need for respect for any decisions taken by women was urged, particularly in the treatment of those women who return to abusive situations. It was argued that they should be treated seriously and with the same respect and care each time they turn up.

Al-Anon/Alcoholics Anonymous (AA)

Eight women went to Al-Anon which provides support for the families of alcohol abusers and to AA which organises group meetings for alcohol abusers and their partners.

There was a mixed reaction to the kind of support women found available when they went to Al-Anon because of their partners drinking problem. Some found it very helpful because by talking to other women, they realised that it was not an individual problem. One woman was helped because *"I could discuss my feelings and get it off my chest."* She said she learned how to cope with alcohol. *"I learned that I had to live my own life and not do things for him."* However, other women were critical of just that positive aspect of the Al-Anon groups. They felt that they were encouraged to stay in the relationship. *"They give you courage to stay and you learn how to cope. But you learn to live with the violence."* One woman criticised this approach: *"They were all a pack of head cases… they thought that you should be able to live with this and put up with this."* She thought it might work for some families if the man was trying to give up the drink. *"But it doesn't really work if you're living with somebody that doesn't want to give the drink up."* These women felt they received no advice on confronting or ending the violence.

This emphasis on coping and putting up with the drink and the violence may have encouraged men to expect support for their behaviour. One woman was encouraged to go to Al-Anon by her husband. His friends and their wives all went to the meeting and he hoped *"they would put me right, as to how to look after him.*

Needless to say, she did not get any information about tackling the violence.

Domestic violence is an issue that is addressed by a wide range of voluntary agencies, community groups and women's organisations. This chapter has demonstrated that these groups are not only filling the gaps, but are also providing a crucial and life-saving response not always available elsewhere. Groups working in local areas represent vital resources and work with currently marginalised and poorly serviced groups of women. Women's Aid is of central importance. It is based on a woman-centred orientation, providing a challenging response and safe environment for abused women. We saw in the previous chapter that some professionals have doubts about the relevance of what Women's Aid can offer, but their experiences in crisis provision, and in building community awareness about domestic violence provide us both with general principles and many suggestions and lessons to be taken up in further work. It is essential that the work of these groups be recognised and supported with adequate funding and that effective liaison between the voluntary and statutory sectors should occur.

Six

Conclusion and Recommendations

Domestic violence is potentially life-threatening, it is directed p‍‍‍‍
marily against women and includes emotional and physical abuse ‍‍
men to dominate and control their female partners. Children a‍‍
also seriously affected both emotionally and physically by this vi‍
lence. A recent report in Great Britain concluded that domest‍
violence was among the most serious of our national social pro‍
lems, important not only for the suffering it caused but for its effe‍
on the community as a whole (Victim Support 1992). The seriou‍
ness of domestic violence was also borne out by the findings of t‍
study, which showed the extent of the problems for both the hel‍
seekers and the help-providers.

This research book documents the impact of domestic violence ‍
the women who are on the receiving end of it. It can threat‍
women's lives and damage their health, both physically and psych‍
logically. Women have been killed, pregnant women have be‍
beaten, women have suffered miscarriages, women have been rap‍
by their partners. Often the women have seen no escape fr‍
the brutality except by inflicting harm on themselves or even
attempting to end their own lives.

It needs to be recognised that leaving a violent relationship ‍
involve difficult decisions for women, particularly where there ‍
children concerned. The research, however, shows that women ‍
not passive victims and once they have made a decision to lea‍
then ways need to be found which empower them to do so. Wom‍
may start the process through their families, mainly their moth‍
but they do look to and use the statutory and voluntary agencies‍
well. There was a high level of contact with the statutory agenc‍
amongst the women we interviewed but there was also, sadly, a ‍
level of helpfulness recorded.

We found that there was a wide range of agencies who were c‍
cerned about the problem of domestic violence. Some of these ‍

already developed good practice in the field. One of the first things, however, which professionals need to recognise is that to even name the problem, let alone seek help for it, is a major issue, particularly in the context of Northern Ireland. Services fell down in the lack of identification of domestic violence especially at the early stage when intervention could be most effective.

There was a good deal of mutual denial and minimisation of abuse amongst some of the professionals. Different models of explanation were put forward by different agencies as well as by the professions within the agencies. When confronted with evidence of domestic violence, some professionals sought to find explanations for it in the conduct of the women whilst others used alcohol abuse or family history as explanatory factors.

In their help-seeking, women were often made to feel that the plight of their children was the only cause for concern. Occasionally, the focus on children and not their own needs in relation to the violence made the women reticent about coming forward in the first place. The outcome, unintentional though it was, was one of double victimisation, once by the abuser and then again by the system to which the women turned for help. It was ironic too that despite this focus on children, there was a lack of services provided for those women who have left violent relationships and had identified a need for on-going support and counselling in relation to their children.

Men need to be challenged about their behaviour when they have been responsible for inflicting abuse on their partners or children. Few agencies are currently addressing this need. There are differences of view both about the priority and nature of this work. Our interviews show, however, that some innovatory developments are being made by more specialised units. By intervening with men who use excuses, such as their alcoholism, to minimise violence, and working with families of abusing men, these units have introduced ways of challenging men's attitudes and enabling women to get some sense of control back into their lives.

Another challenge is the whole question of the centrality of domestic violence for professional practice and more specifically the crossover between the guidelines which have already been developed on child abuse to domestic violence. The research shows that although there are similarities between the issues, there also needs to be a difference in approach. It could well be that, in the case of domestic violence, those protective services which are the basis of child abuse interventions need to be supplemented or even replaced with services that facilitate women's sense of empowerment and autonomy.

The question of whether there was a special 'Northern Ireland dimension' to domestic violence was an important theme of the study and the research has identified specific problems for the help-seeking process in Northern Ireland which serve to keep domestic violence hidden. Marriage and the family have a particularly central importance to women's lives in Northern Ireland. The social and religious attitudes which stigmatise lone parents are barriers which women must overcome before they step onto the help-seeking ladder. Public attention emphasising the violence resulting from the 'Troubles' makes it more difficult to attract the necessary resources and public concern for the problems associated with other forms of violence.

There are also the additional needs of specific groups within Northern Ireland. Women living in rural areas, Traveller women and Asian women all have specific problems which need to be addressed. The lack of police response poses specific problems for women living in nationalist areas when looking for support in crisis situations. The particular needs of elderly women and disabled women living with violent partners are further issues which must be considered by help providers.

Clearly the problem is complex and requires solutions that are multi-faceted. Any consideration of domestic violence must be placed in the context of the continued inequality of women in the family and in wider society. Women's lack of opportunities in work and in education contribute to inequality generally between men and women. In addition, government policies in relation to housing, welfare, and childcare impact on women's ability to leave violent homes and begin independent lives. Societal attitudes which condone rather than condemn this violence serve only to perpetuate this abuse in the long-term. Lack of opportunities and societal attitudes demand a challenging and long-term response by all concerned with the issue.

The major concern of the research, however, has been with health and social service professionals and it is these who are the focus of the recommendations listed below. Underlying the recommendations are three key assumptions:

- of *consistency* in the treatment of women who have suffered from domestic violence
- of the *maintenance* of the dignity of women when services are offered
- of *respect* for the ability of women to make their own decisions, but coupled with an appreciation of (a) the difficulties of this decision-making, and (b) the effect of depression on people's decision-making processes.

These assumptions underlie the philosophy which, as we have seen, has been articulated in some detail by Women's Aid in its long history of provision for women who have been abused.

Where does the question of costs and cost effectiveness fit? Some of the changes can be made with minimal financial input. Others however require resources for new initiatives and the extension of those already in existence. Such costs need to be placed in the context of the multiple agencies currently dealing with the problem as it gets passed on, either deliberately or unintentionally, from one agency to the next.

Below we set out a series of 13 recommendations. Some of these are covered in more detail in Annex 3. It must be remembered that this study was initiated as a preliminary to an intervention project by the DHSS to alleviate the problems of domestic violence in Northern Ireland. There is no doubt that there is a demonstrable need for such a project. Both the seriousness and the urgency of the problems are now apparent. They demand an urgent response.

Recommendations

Recommendation 1

A *multi-disciplinary conference* be arranged to disseminate the findings to the various professions, agencies and participants involved in the research. Individual conferences for professional groups and Area Board conferences should also be arranged for dissemination purposes and for the development of position statements on domestic violence.

Recommendation 2

A *central policy* be developed by government departments in Northern Ireland to enable a coherent and coordinated framework on domestic violence to be put in place.

Recommendation 3

A *Northern Ireland Working Party* be established, involving statutory and voluntary agencies, to address the specific issues highlighted by this research and to facilitate the development of policy and guidelines on domestic violence. (This could build on the work of the Working Party on Domestic Violence and the Law, see Annex 4, Women's Aid).

Recommendation 4

Codes of practice be designed for identifying and recording domestic violence.

Recommendation 5

A framework be developed for the *collection of statistics* on domestic violence by social work, health and medical agencies. Mechanisms should also be developed which provide clear recognition of domestic violence within criminal statistics.

Recommendation 6

Single disciplinary courses on domestic violence be introduced as an integral part of pre- and post-qualifying education together with in-service training programmes within each professional group.

Recommendation 7

Multi-disciplinary training programmes be developed within the context of the help-seeking process in Northern Ireland (see Annex 3.1).

Recommendation 8

A community-based advocacy, information and advice service be established as a pilot project in Northern Ireland; this should include a 24-hour crisis help-line (see Annex 3.2).

Recommendation 9

Aftercare, support and counselling services for women be established, dealing also with the needs of children who have witnessed or experienced domestic violence (see Annex 3.3).

Recommendation 10

Local inter-agency domestic violence forums be resourced and extended to develop greater liaison between statutory and voluntary agencies at the community level (see Annex 3.4).

Recommendation 11

A programme of public education be developed in schools and community youth work settings to challenge the use of violence in intimate relationships (see Annex 3.5).

Recommendation 12

Work with abusers be extended, drawing lessons from evaluations elsewhere (see Annex 3.6).

Recommendation 13

Areas for future research should be identified and funded to address the gaps in the current knowledge on domestic violence (see Annex 3.7).

Further Details of the Samples

1. *Sample of Helpseekers (n = 56)*

The women in the sample were referred or reached through the following:

Women's Aid	24	Personal Contacts	3
Women's groups and centres	10	Social Workers	3
Community groups/workers	7	Housing Executive	2
Solicitors	6	Sydenham House	1

2. *Sample of Help-Providers (n = 120)*

Statutory Sector

EASTERN BOARD: Manager; Director of Social Services; Unit Manager, Family and Child Care

WESTERN BOARD: Unit General Manager

HEALTH AND SOCIAL SERVICES PROFESSIONALS:

Urban Area: Social Workers; GPs; Health Visitors; Alcohol Abuse Unit; Mental Health Team (Community Psychiatric Nurses, Social Workers); Family Centre (Social Workers); Accident and Emergency Departments

Rural Area: Social Workers; GPs; Health Visitors; Mental Health Team (Doctor, Social Workers); Community Nurses; Accident and Emergency Department

HOUSING EXECUTIVE

Urban Area: Manager; Homeless Advice Unit; Hostel Managers

Rural Area: Manager

ROYAL ULSTER CONSTABULARY:

Urban Area: Operational Research

Rural Area: RUC Care Unit

PROBATION SERVICE

Voluntary Sector

Urban Area: Women's Group; Women's Centres; Victim Support; Chinese Welfare Association

Rural Area: Community Centres; Clergy; Catholic Marriage Guidance; Gingerbread; ACE Centre

HEADQUARTERS STAFF:

Northern Ireland Women's Aid Federation ; Sydenham House ; Relate ; Catholic Marriage Advisory Council ; Samaritans ; Safer Towns ; Gingerbread ; Rape Crisis Centre

Women's Experiences of Domestic Violence: Tables

TABLE 1
Geographical Spread of Sample of Women

West Belfast	13 (3 from Traveller community)
North Belfast	5
Lisburn	6
Poleglass	5
East Belfast	4
Derry	4
Armagh	3
Bangor	2
Ballymena	2
Antrim	1
Ballykelly	1
Carrickfergus	1
Carrickmore	1
Craigavon	1
Dungiven	1
Fermanagh	1
Glenarm	1
Gortin	1
Limavady	1
Omagh	1
Strabane	1

TABLE 2
When Violence Started

Early in Relationship	No.
Start of relationship	15
Early in relationship	7
Before marriage	2
Night of marriage	2
3–6 months after marriage	6
During first year	2
First pregnancy or birth	3
One year after	2
2–3 years into relationship	3
Total	42

Later in Relationship	
Last half	1
Last few years	2
The last year	1
Total	4

No answer	10
Overall Total	56

TABLE 3
Years in Violent Relationship

	No.
1–5	19
6–10	15
11–15	4
16–20	6
over 20	2
Total	46
no answer	10
Overall Total	56

TABLE 4
First Contact in Response to Violence

	No.
1. Family	
Woman's family	37
Mother only	11
Sister only	7
Family in general	19
Husband's family	2
Total	39
2. Professional Agency	
(Statutory and Voluntary)	
Social worker	
Housing Executive	
Marriage guidance	
Women's Aid	
Health visitor	
Doctor	
Army Welfare	
Total	10
3. Other informal	
Friends	2
Neighbour	2
Total	4
4. No response	3
Overall Total	56

TABLE 5
What Did Women Do When Violence Occurred?

First Time		Worst Time		Last Time	
Nothing	26	Hospital	8	Left	40
Talked to family	10	Nothing	9	Solicitor	4
Police	1	Ran out of house	3	Police	3
Doctor	1	Police	4	Nothing	3
Neighbour	1	Family	5	Not app.	3
Marriage guidance	1	Solicitor	2	Overdose	1
Housing Executive	1	Overdose	2	Encouraged	
Rang Women's Aid	1	Attacked him	2	new rel.	1
Left the house	1	Social worker	1	Social worker	1
Went to a refuge	1	Army welfare	1		
No response	12	Doctor	1		
		Left (& went back)	2		
		No response	16		
Total	56		56		56

For eight women, the worse incident was the last. Their responses are recorded under "last time". Three of these left, three went to solicitors for separation and Protection and Exclusion orders. The other two went to the police and a doctor.

TABLE 6
First Contact for Women Who Left Home

	No.
Family	14
Housing Executive	6
Social worker	6
Refuge	4
Police	3
Solicitors	3
Doctor	1
England	1
Community group	1
Total	40

TABLE 7
Reasons Given by Women for not Acting Sooner
(based on multiple responses)

Reason Given	No. of Responses	%
Attitudes of shame, pride, self-blame	18	32
Concern for the children	16	29
Fear of partner	13	23
Expectations for change	10	18
Objective factors - information, money	8	14
Attitudes to marriage	7	13
Fear of family reaction	7	13
Feelings for partner	3	5
Learned to live with it	3	5

TABLE 8
Statutory Agencies Contacted by Women

Agency	Contacts		No. described as helpful		No. described as not helpful	
	No.	%	No.	%	No.	%
Social Workers	36	64	10	28	26	72
Housing Executive	36	64	15	42	21	58
Police	35	63	9	26	26	74
GPs		30	54		9	30
21	70					
Health Visitors	25	45	4	16	21	84
Accident and Emergency	22	39	5	23	17	77
Alcohol Abuse Units	6	11	2	33	4	67
CPNs	5	9	2	40	3	60
Political Representatives	5	9	4	80	1	20
Midwives	2	4	–	0	2	100
Probation	2	4	–	0	2	100
Army Welfare	2	4	–	0	2	100
Teacher	1	2	1	100	–	0

Percentages are based on 56 interviewees.
Table is based on multiple agency contacts

TABLE 9
Voluntary Agencies (other than Women's Aid)
Contacted by Women

Agency	Contacts No.	%	No. described as Helpful	No. described as Not Helpful
Al-Anon/AA	8	14	4	4
Samaritans	6	11	6	–
Rape Crisis Centre	3	5	2	1
Women's Groups	2	4	2	–
Citizens Advice Bureau	2	4	2	–
Well Woman Clinic	1	2	1	–
Gamblers Anonymous	1	2	1	–
Mother/Toddler Group	1	2	1	–
Vincent de Paul	1	2	1	–
Ulidia	1	2	1	–
NSPCC	1	2	1	–

Percentages are based on 56 interviewees
Table is based on multiple agency contacts

ANNEX 3

Suggestions for D.H.S.S. Interventions on Domestic Violence

A range of possible interventions is set out here which could be considered at different levels of management and by different service delivery groups.

3.1 Training

Multi-disciplinary training should be carried out with the relevant personnel from health and social services, Housing Executive, the Probation Service and the Royal Ulster Constabulary as well as with the voluntary agencies referred to in this study. The production of *training packs* for professionals working in health and social agencies building on work carried out elsewhere, but also related to the findings of this study which point to the distinctive help-seeking process of women in certain areas of Northern Ireland. A video which would accompany these training packs should also be produced to familiarise professionals with recent legislative changes clarify their role in relation to the work of the more specialised agencies and illustrate the facilities which are currently available in refuges and other types of hostel accommodation.

3.2 Community Based Unit

The establishment of a pilot *community based domestic violence project* to provide a specific service for advice, practical assistance and information for both abused women and professionals in the voluntary and statutory sectors. It would include a crisis service as part of its work and would introduce a 24-hour helpline to provide the specialist backup for frontline agencies such as Women's Aid and the Samaritans. In an evaluation of a Domestic Violence Crisis Service in Canberra, Australia, the 24-hour crisis service was one of the most effective ways of responding to the immediate needs of women experiencing domestic violence (see Hopkins and McGregor

1991:44-64). Within Northern Ireland, the need for such a service has also been identified by the RUC. This project would also act as a broker service in enabling other agencies to make appropriate referrals and serve as a liaison between the statutory and voluntary sectors. For women who have been identified as unlikely to seek refuge accommodation, it would act as a community alternative. It would be responsible for short term support and counselling and link with a local Women's Centre in organising assertiveness and personal development classes for women who have experienced domestic violence.

3.3   Aftercare

The establishment of an *after-care programme* to provide advice and information as well as a counselling service for women and children who have left violent relationships but still need help for their current problems. It would involve home-visits and networking between women and children and draw on the expertise currently available in the voluntary and statutory sectors. It could be developed on an outreach basis and would have a childcare worker and/or a child psychologist with expertise in this field attached to the programme. Women's Aid have developed several aftercare projects to date and are in the best position to develop this work further in Northern Ireland.

Suggestions for Other Interventions on Domestic Violence in Northern Ireland

3.4   The establishment of *domestic violence forums* in local areas to specifically address the needs of women living in the community, to raise public awareness on domestic violence and to improve communication and liaison between the statutory and voluntary agencies. These forums could also be used to develop joint protocols on domestic violence in the local areas. Such forums should be adequately resourced and rather than being set up on an ad hoc basis they should instead draw on the experience and expertise of Women's Aid in this field. Specific funding should be allocated to Women's Aid in order to facilitate this process.

3.5   The development of a programme of public education in schools and community youth work settings to challenge the use of violence in personal relationships. Information could be provided on help-provision and on legal rights as part of a training package targeted at this group. Training for teachers and youth workers would also be a major focus of this public education programme.

3.6   The extension of work with abusers, particularly where these are drawing on the evaluation of similar work elsewhere. The CHANGE project in Scotland provides a court-mandated re-education pro-gramme for abusive men and is currently under evaluation. Such projects should seek to maintain contact with the offender's partner in order to ensure her protection and safety.

3.7   The identification and funding of action research projects to address the gaps in the current knowledge on domestic violence particularly in rural communities and in the areas of civil and criminal justice, housing, and policy in Northern Ireland.

ANNEX 4

Initiatives on Domestic Violence in Northern Ireland and Elsewhere

Recent Initiatives on Domestic Violence in Northern Ireland

1991 and 1992 have also proved to be important years for raising the profile attached to domestic violence in Northern Ireland. Whilst this research was being carried out, a number of local initiatives on domestic violence were, or are about to be, introduced by different service providers in the field. Some of these are currently being evaluated, however, and it should not be assumed that all of these initiatives will be retained in the longer term.

Women's Aid

In addition to the current initiatives noted in this report, Women's Aid are also setting up a regional helpline and local initiatives to provide a more comprehensive and structured support service to abused women in the community, particularly for those women wishing to remain in and improve the relationship. A more developed aftercare service has also been established for women and children leaving the refuge setting in order to support them through this vulnerable period. An additional 145 bed spaces are being planned over the next five years by upgrading and extending an existing refuge in Belfast and the establishment of new refuges in Craigavon, Lisburn and Ballymena.

Women's Aid also launched its first public campaign on domestic violence in December 1992. Large posters and billboards carrying eye-catching slogans such as "When home is where the hurt is" and "Sealed with a fist" were used to convey their message that domestic violence is an extensive problem and needs to be publicly challenged.

Working Party On Domestic Violence

In Northern Ireland, in 1992, a report on Domestic Violence and the Law was also published. This arose out of a conference organised by Women's Aid and the Northern Ireland Solicitor Family Law Association and was specifically concerned with the problems encountered by victims of domestic violence in the civil and criminal justice system. Responding to a conference recommendation, the Domestic Violence Working Group has been set up with representatives from Women's Aid, Social Services, R.U.C. and the Solicitors Family Law Association with a view to initiating multi-agency action.

Newtownabbey Domestic Violence Forum

The Newtownabbey Domestic Violence Forum is the first community initiative on domestic violence in Northern Ireland. It has been introduced by the Safer Towns Initiative managed by the Extern Organisation, a registered charity concerned with crime prevention and community initiatives and has utilised the resources of Women's Aid at the relevant stages of its development. Safer Towns is managed by the Northern Ireland Office and is aligned to the Safer Cities programme run by the Home Office in England and Wales.

The Domestic Violence Forum was set up on an interagency basis following a seminar on domestic violence in Newtownabbey in February, 1992. The Forum is made up of representatives of 13 local statutory and voluntary agencies who have agreed the following objectives:

to promote awareness on domestic violence at the local level;

to reduce the incidence of domestic violence;

to ensure the provision and delivery of high quality services to those at risk; and

to improve communication and information systems between the statutory and voluntary agencies in the local community.

To date, an information leaflet has been published providing information on basic services and legal rights and lists the contact numbers for organisations such as Women's Aid. It also provides information on the local sources of help such as the Housing Executive, the social services, the police and others. Public places such as libraries, community centres and the reception areas of doctors and dentists surgeries as well as the local hospital have been targetted for the distribution of these leaflets.

Training has been organised for front-line staff in the local Housing Executive and an information pack aimed at doctors, health visitors, advice workers, counsellors, solicitors and other professionals is currently being prepared. The Forum is also organising seminars, talks and information sessions on domestic violence in the local estates.

Lisburn Domestic Violence Forum

In June 1992 the Lisburn Women's Support Network, which represents women's groups from Lisburn, Poleglass, Twinbrook and Seymour Hill, organised a conference on domestic violence. The women brought together a range of statutory and voluntary personnel to explain to local women what services the agencies were providing in relation to domestic violence. The initiative has led to the start of a Lisburn Domestic Violence Forum consisting of 12 statutory and voluntary organisations which operate in the Lisburn area.

Royal Ulster Constabulary

The R.U.C. have introduced two pilot projects in Northern Ireland, alongside the appointment of Divisional Domestic Violence Liaison Officers following the introduction of the Force Order on Domestic Violence in Northern Ireland in 1991.

One of the projects has introduced follow-up calls to women who are still in relationships and have made contact with the police as a consequence of physical violence by their partners. A female police officer has been assigned the task of returning to women when the initial crisis has passed to see what further help can be facilitated. The project is on-going and is currently being evaluated.

The second project involves issuing cards to women who have requested assistance from the local police. This card lists the telephone numbers of the agencies dealing with domestic violence together with a contact number for the relevant housing executive office in the local area. This project is also being evaluated at present.

Probation Service

Two probation officers are developing a project in conjunction with a local Women's Centre in South Belfast. This will include a men's group which is being established as part of an initiative to challenge male attitudes on domestic violence in the local area. The project is being designed as a community based response to the problem. It has included other agencies such as the police in its initial discussion of the project and has visited other projects of a similar type elsewhere. The Association of Chief Officers of Probation is in the process of agreeing national guidelines on domestic violence for probation services.

Gingerbread

Gingerbread introduced a Teens Project in 1992 to facilitate the specialist support which teenagers of single parents had identified as one of their needs in dealing with the effects of previous experience of domestic violence in their lives. A need for similar work with younger children has also been identified, as well as more specialist support for single parents who feel that they are having to deal alone with the effects of the violence on their children.

Initiatives Elsewhere on Domestic Violence

Guidelines for the Medical Profession

The Royal College of General Practitioners and the British Association of Accident and Emergency Medicine are currently producing guidelines on domestic violence.

Lake Louise Declaration

Issued in May 1990 by the Federal, Provincial and Territorial Ministers responsible for the status of women in Canada, this central policy on violence against women is an example of goverments informing public opinion, creating a statement of intent and agreeing a set of principles to guide statutory activities.

Leeds Inter-Agency Forum

Set up following recommendations from the West Yorkshire research and funded by the City Council, this Forum brings agencies and groups together, to share information and to develop policies and practices to make responses to women more consistent across the city. The Forum involves a wide range of people, has created a directory of information and information pack, multi-lingual posters, policy development in agencies, and training initiatives. It has focused on supporting the development of a Black Women's Forum and a local pilot programme of integrated service delivery in a specific community in Leeds. Similar fora exist in Nottinghamshire, Wolverhampton, Gloucestershire, Keighley (Yorkshire), Newham (London), Tottenham (London) and other areas.

Duluth, Minnesota: Domestic Abuse Intervention Project

This 10 year old project is considered a national model of coordinated community action against domestic violence in the USA. Instigated by the local women's shelter in Duluth, Minnesota, it encompasses coordinated policies amongst the criminal justice agencies, a court mandated men's programme, a wide range of support groups and services for women and public education and training campaigns. The Domestic Violence Intervention Project in Hammersmith is based on this project.

Hammersmith and Fulham Council

The Council has prioritised work on domestic violence within its Community Safety Strategy. The Council has developed a Corporate Programme involving all departments which include new policies, procedures, training, staff support, advice and information, and public education. It services the multi-agency Domestic Violence Forum which seeks to improve and coordinate services across the borough,and has supported the development of a new project of separate programmes for women survivors and male perpetrators.

Glasgow Women's Support Project

This project acts as a community based resource centre and networking group for professionals and community people seeking to challenge the abuse of women and children. It specifically acts to break down the barriers between professionals, survivors and others in the community via training and outreach work. It has conducted survey research with the local newspaper, developed self defence initiatives for women with disabilities and is branching out into safety projects.

Victim Support

In July 1992, Victim Support published the report of a national inter-agency working party on domestic violence. Victim Support is a national charity which counsels victims of crime. It convened this working party as a result of a substantially increasing demand for support from victims of domestic violence both in Great Britain and in Northern Ireland. The report recommends that a single government department should be responsible for ensuring that agencies work effectively together and points to the establishment of domestic violence forums as being an effective intervention in this area.

Police Statistics on Incidents of Domestic Violence

Reported Incidents of Domestic Violence, 1-4-91 to 31-3-92, Northern Ireland			
Division	Incidents Reported	Population	Incidents/ 10,000 Population
A	212	95,630	22.2
B	209	136,750	15.3
D	629	240,700	26.1
E	288	175,010	16.4
G	162	138,280	11.7
H	85	112,050	7.6
J	195	125,550	15.5
K	107	70,580	15.2
L	242	109,780	22.0
N	206	128,210	16.1
O	176	116.080	15.2
P	329	120,140	27.4
Northern Ireland	2840	1,568,740	18.1

See map overleaf

POLICE STATISTICS ON INCIDENTS OF DOMESTIC VIOLENCE

Reported Incidents of Domestic Violence, 1-4-91 to 31-3-92, Northern Ireland

Division	Incidents Reported	Population	Incidents/ 10,000 Population
A	212	95,630	22.2
B	209	136,750	15.3
D	629	240,700	26.1
E	288	175,010	16.4
G	162	138,280	11.7
H	85	112,050	7.6
J	195	125,550	15.5
K	107	70,580	15.2
L	242	109,780	22.0
N	206	128,210	16.1
O	176	116.080	15.2
P	329	120,140	27.4
Northern Ireland	2840	1,568,740	18.1

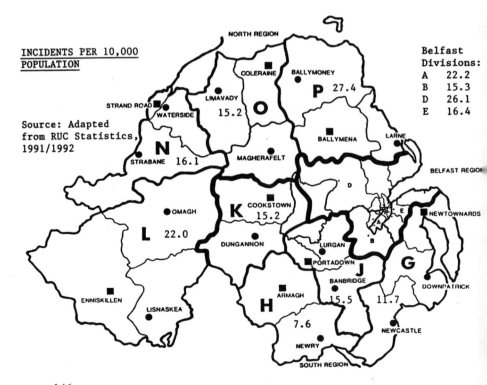

INCIDENTS PER 10,000 POPULATION

Source: Adapted from RUC Statistics, 1991/1992

Belfast
Divisions:
A   22.2
B   15.3
D   26.1
E   16.4

Bibliography

Ardoyne Women's Research Project (1992), *Unheard Voices: Women's Needs in Ardoyne*, Belfast: Regency Press.

Atkins, S and Hoggett, B (1984), *Women and the Law*, London: Blackwells.

Berk, R, Newton, P and Berk, S (1986), 'What a difference a day makes: an empirical study of the impact of shelters for battered women', *Journal of Marriage and the Family*, 48:481–491.

Bergman, B and Brismar, B (1992), 'Family Violence is a Learned Behaviour', *Journal of Public Health*, 106:45–52.

Binney, V et al. (1981), *Leaving Violent Men: A Study of Refuges and Housing for Battered Women*, Bristol: Women's Aid Federation, England.

Borkowski, M et al. (1983), *Marital Violence: the community response*, London: Tavistock Publications.

Bowker, C et al. (1988), 'On the Relationship Between Wife Beating and Child Abuse' pp 158–174 in K Yllo and M Bograd (eds), *Feminist Perspectives on Child Abuse*, London: Sage.

Bowker, C H and Maurer, L (1987), 'The Medical Treatment of Battered Wives', 12:25–45.

Breines, W and Gordon, L (1984), 'The New Scholarship on Family Violence', *Signs*, 8:490–531.

Browne, A (1987), *When Battered Women Kill*, New York: The Free Press.

Browne, A and Williams, K R (1989), 'Exploring the effect of resource availability and the likelihood of female-perpetrated homicides' *Law Society Review*, 23:75–94.

Browning, J and Dutton, D (1986), 'Assessment of Wife Assault with the Conflicts Tactics Scale, *Journal of Marriage and the Family*, 48:375–379.

Burge, S K (1989), 'Violence against Women as a Health Care Issue', *Family Medicine*, 21:368–373.

Casey, M (1989), *Domestic Violence Against Women: The Women's Perspective*, Dublin: Social Psychology Research Unit, U.C.D.

Council on Ethical and Judical Affairs, American Medical Association (1992), 'Physicians and domestic violence: ethical considerations', *J.A.M.A.*, 267:3190–3193.

Council of Scientific Affairs, American Medical Association (1992), 'Violence against women; Relevance for Medical Practitioners', *J.A.M.A.*, 267:3184–3189.

Davies, D (1991), 'Intervention with Male Toddlers who have Witnessed Parental Violence' *Families in Society*, 73:515–524.

Dobash, R E and Dobash, R (1979), *Violence Against Wives*, New York: The Free Press.

Dobash, R E and Dobash, R P (1984), 'The Nature and Antecedents of Violent Events', *British Journal of Criminology*, 24(3):269–288.

Dobash, R E and Dobash, R (1992), *Women, Violence and Social Change*, London: Routledge.

Dobash, R E, Dobash, R and Cavanagh, D C (1985), 'The Contact between battered women and social and medical agencies', in J Pahl (ed), *Private Violence and Public Policy*, London: Routledge & Kegan.

Dobash, R, Dobash, R E, Wilson and Daly (1992), 'The Myth of the Asymmetrical Nature of Domestic Violence', *Social Problems*, 39(1):402–432.

Douglas, M A (1987), 'The Battered Women Syndrome', in D J Sonkin (ed), *Domestic Violence on Trial*, New York: Springer Publishing Company.

Edwards, S (1986a), *The Police Response to Domestic Violence in London*, London: Central London Polytechnic.

Edwards, S (1986b), 'The Real Risks of Violence Behind Closed Doors', *New Law Journal*, 136/628:1191–1193.

Edwards, S (1989), *Policing Domestic Violence*, London: Sage.

Elman, R and Edwards, M (1991), 'Unprotected by the Swedish Welfare State', *Women's Studies International Forum*, 14(5):413–421.

Evason, E (1982), *Hidden Violence, A Study of Battered Women in Northern Ireland*, Belfast: Farset Press.

Fagan, R, Barnett, O and Patton, J (1988), 'Reasons for Alcohol Use in Maritally Violent Men', *American Journal of Drug and Alcohol Abuse*, 14(3):371–392.

Flitcraft, A (1992), 'Violence, Values and Gender', *J.A.M.A.*, 267:3194–3195.

Freeman, M D A (1979), *Violence in the Home*, Farmborough: Saxon House.

Frieze, I H (1983), 'Investigating the causes and consequences of marital rape', *Signs*, 8(3):532–553.

Freize, I H and Browne, A (1989), 'Violence In Marriage', in L Ohlin and M Tonry (eds), *Family Violence*, Chicago: University of Chicago Press.

Friedman, J et al (1992), 'Inquiry about Victimization Experiences: A Survey of Patient Preferences and Physician Practices', *Archives Intern Medicine*, 152:1186–1190.

Gayford, J J (1975), 'Wife Battering: A Preliminary Survey of 100 Cases', *British Medical Journal*, Jan.:194–197.

Gelles, R J and Conte, J R (1990), 'Domestic Violence and Sexual Abuse of Children: A review of Research in the Eighties', *Journal of Marriage and Family*, 52:1045–1058.

Gelles, R J and Cornell, C (1985), *Intimate Violence in Families*, California: Sage.

Gelles, R and Harrop, J (1989), 'Violence and psychological distress among women', *Journal of Interpersonal Violence*, 4:400–420.

Gelles, R J and Straus, M (1988), *Intimate Violence*, New York: Simon and Schuster.

Gin, N E et al. (1990), 'Prevalence of Domestic Violence in Ambulatory Medicine Patients', *Journal of Clinical Research*, 38(2):694.

Graham, P, Rawlings, E and Rimini, W (1988), 'Survivors of Terror: Battered Women, Hostages and the Stockholm Syndrome' in K Yllo and M Bograd (eds), op cit.

Hanmer, J (1985), 'Violence to Women: From Private Sorrow to public issue', in G Ashworth and L Bonnerjea (eds), *The Invisible Decade: UK Women in the United Nations Decade 1976–1986*, Aldershot: Gower.

Hammer, J and Maynard, M (eds) (1987), *Women, Violence and Social Control*, London: Macmillan.

Hanmer, J, Radford, J and Stanko, E (1989), *Women, Policing and Male Violence: International Perspectives*, London: Routledge.

Hanmer, J and Saunders, S (1984), *Well Founded Fear*, London: Hutchinson.

Harris, R N and Bologh, R W (1985), 'The dark side of love: blue and white collar wife abuse', *Victimology*, 10:242–252.

Helton, A, Anderson, E and McFarlane, J (1987), 'Battered and Pregnant: A prevalence Study', *American Journal of Public Health*, 77:166–174.

Hester, M and Radford, L (1992), 'Domestic Violence and Access Arrangements for Children in Denmark and Britain', *Journal of Social Welfare and Family Law*, 1.

Hoff, C A (1990), *Battered Women As Survivors*, Routledge: London.

Jaffe, P, Wolfe, D and Kaye, S (1990), *Children of Battered Women*, Newbury Park, CA: Sage.

Johnson, H (1989), 'Wife Assault in Canada', paper presented at the Annual Conference of the American Society of Criminology, cited in R B Dobash and R Dobash (1992), *Women, Violence and Social Change*.

Johnson, I (1992), 'Economic, Situational and Psychological Correlates of the Decision Making Process of Battered Women', *Families in Society*, 73:168–176.

Johnson, N (ed) (1985), *Marital Violence*, London: Routledge and Kegan.

Kaufman Kantor, G and Straus, M A (1987), 'The Drunken Bum Theory of Wife Battering', *Social Problems*, 34:213–230

Kelly, L (1988), *Surviving Sexual Violence*, Cambridge: Polity Press.

Kelly, L (1992), 'Towards an Integrated Community Response to Domestic Violence', Paper presented to the Hartlepool Safer Cities Conference on Women and Safety.

Kelly, L and Radford, J (1991), 'Nothing Really Happened', *Critical Social Policy*, 30:39–53.

Kurz, D (1989), 'Social Science Perspectives on Wife Abuse', *Gender and Society*, 3(4):489–505.

Kurz, D and Stark, E (1988), 'Not so benign neglect: the medical response to battering', in K Yllo and M Bograd (eds), *Feminist Perspectives on Wife Abuse*, London: Sage.

Langley, P A (1991), 'Family Violence: Towards a family-oriented Public Policy', *Families in Society*, 73:574–576.

Levinson, D (1989), *Family Violence in Cross-Cultural Perspective*, London: Sage.

McFarlane, J et al (1992), 'Assessing for Abuse during pregnancy', *J.A.M.A.*, 267:3176–3178.

McGibbon, A, Cooper, C and Kelly, C (1989), *What Support?*, London: Hammersmith and Fulham Council, Community and Police Committee.

McGregor, H and Hopkins, A (1991), *Working for Change: The Movement Against Domestic Violence*, Sydney: Allen and Unwin.

McIlwaine, G (1989), 'Women Victims of Domestic Violence', *Brit. Medical Journal*, 299:995–996.

McLaughlin, E (forthcoming), 'Women and the Family in Northern Ireland', in M Crozier and G MacFarlane (eds), *Northern Ireland: Culture and Society*.

Mama, A (1989), *The Hidden Struggle: Statutory and Voluntary Sector Responses to Violence against Black Women in the Home*, London: Race and Housing Research Unit.

Maguire, S (1988), '"Sorry Love" – Violence against women in the home and the state response', *Critical Social Policy*, 23.

Marzmuk, P et al (1992), 'The Epidemiology of Murder-Suicide', *Journal of American Medical Association*, 267:3179–3183.

Maynard, M (1985), 'The Response of Social Workers to domestic violence' in J Pahl (ed), *Private Violence and Public Policy*, London: Routledge and Kegan.

Mederos, M (1987), 'Theorizing Continuities and Discontinuities Between Normal Men and Abusive Men', Paper presented at the Third National Violence Research Conference. New Hampshire.

Montgomery, P (1991), 'Police Response to Wife Assault in Northern Ireland', *Victimology*.

Montgomery, P and Bell, V (1986), *Police Response to Wife Assault: A Northern Ireland Study*, Belfast: Women's Aid Federation.

Montgomery, P and Davies, C (1991), 'A Woman's Place in Northern Ireland', *in* P Stringer and G Robinson (eds), *Social Attitudes in Northern Ireland*, Belfast: Blackstaff Press.

Northern Ireland Housing Executive (1992), *The Executive's Housing Strategy 1993–96*, Belfast: NIHE.

Northern Ireland Women's Aid Federation (1992), *Domestic Violence and the Law*, conference report, Belfast: Women's Aid.

Oppenlander, N (1982), 'Coping or Copping Out? Police Service Delivery in Domestic Disputes', *Criminology*, 20(3–4):449–465.

Orr, J (1984), 'Violence Against Women', *Nursing Times*, April 25, 34–36.

Pagelow, M (1981), *Women-battering: Victims and their experience*. Newbury Park, CA: Sage.

Pahl, J (ed) (1985), *Private Violence and Public Policy*, London: Routledge and Kegan.

Pang, L E (1991), *Sociological Study of Chinese Immigrants in Belfast*. Jordanstown: University of Ulster.

Parnas, R (1971), 'The Police Discretion and Diversion of Incidents of Intra-family Violence', *Law and Contemporary Problems*, 36(4): 539–565.

Ptacek, J (1988), 'Why do men batter their wives?', in K Yllo and M Bograd (eds), *Feminist Perspectives on Wife Abuse*, London: Sage.

Roy, M (ed) (1982), *The Abusive Partner*, New York: Van Nostrand Reinhold.

Ruddle, H and O'Connor, J (1992), *Breaking The Silence – Violence In the Home: The Women's Perspective*, Limerick: Mid-Western Health Board.

Russell, D (1982), *Rape in Marriage*, New York: Macmillan.

Sampselle, C (1992), *Violence Against Women: Nursing Research, Education and Practice Issues*, New York: Hemisphere.

Schechter, S (1982), *Women and Male Violence*, Boston: South End Press.

Schechter, S (1992), 'Women's Reactions to the Label Battered: Rethinking ways to Reach Abused Women', Unpublished paper.

Shepherd, J (1990), 'Victims of Personal Violence: The Relevance of Symond's model of Psychological Response and Loss-Theory', *British Journal of Social Work*, 20:309–332.

Shepard, M (1991), 'Feminist Practice Principles for Social Work Intervention in Wife Abuse', *Affilia*, 62(2):87–93.

Smith, L (1989), *Domestic Violence: Home Office Research Study 107*, London: H.M.S.O.

Stanko, E (1985), *Intimate Intrusions. Women's Experience of Male Violence*, London: Routledge and Kegan.

Stark, F and Flitcraft, A (1985), 'Women Battering, Child Abuse and Social Heredity: What is the Relationship', in N Johnson (ed), *Marital Violence*, London: Routledge and Kegan.

Stark, F and Flitcraft, A (1988), 'Violence among intimates: an epidemiological Review', in V B Van Hasselt et al (eds), *Handbook of Family Violence*, New York: Plenum Press.

Stark, F, Flitcraft, A and Frazier, W (1979), 'Medicine and patriarchal violence: The social construction of a private event', *International Journal of Health Services*, 9:461–493.

Straus, M A and Gelles, R J (1986), 'Societal Change and Change in Family Violence from 1975–1985 as revealed by two National Surveys', *Journal of Marriage and the Family*, 48:465–479.

Straus, M A and Gelles, R J (eds) (1990), *Physical Violence in American Families: Risk Factors and Adaptions to Violence in 8,145 Families*, New Jersey: Transaction Publishers.

Straus, M A, Gelles, R J and Steinmetz, S K (1980), *Behind Closed Doors*, New York: Anchor.

Sugg, N K and Inui, T (1992), 'Primary Care Physicians' response to domestic violence: Opening pandora's box', J.A.M.A., 267:3157–3160.

Victim Support (1992), *Domestic Violence: Report of a National Inter-Agency Working Party*, London: Victim Support.

Walker, L E (1979), *The Battered Woman*, New York: Harper and Row.

Walker, L E (1984), *The Battered Women Syndrome*, New York: Springer Press.

Warshaw, C (1989), 'Limitations of the Medical Model in the Care of Battered women'. *Gender and Society*, 3(4):506–517.

White, L (1992), 'Domestic Violence Out of the Closet?', *Brit. Medical Journal*, 305:211–212.

Worrall, S and Pease, K (1986), 'Personal Crime Against Women: Evidence from the 1982 British "Crime Survey"', *Howard Journal*, 25(2):118–124.

Yllo K (1988) 'Political and Methodological Debates in Wife Abuse Research' in K Yllo and M Bograd (eds), *Feminist Perspectives on Wife Abuse*, London: Sage.

Yllo, K and Bograd, M (eds) (1988), *Feminist Perspectives on Wife Abuse*, London: Sage.